SCA Publication Program in Education and Instructional Development

Pamela J. Cooper, Editor
Northwestern University

The SCA Program in Education and Instructional Development supports the Speech Communication Association mission of promoting the study, criticism, research, teaching, and application of artistic, humanistic, and scientific principles of communication. Specifically, the goal of this publication program is to disseminate useful information to teachers and researchers addressing a broad range of issues. The program encompasses multiple theoretical perspectives, research methodologies, and pragmatic experiences. All materials published within this program are peer reviewed by experts selected by the Program Editor.

C-SPAN

In 1979, the cable industry created the Cable-Satellite Public Affairs Network to provide live, gavel-to-gavel coverage of the U.S. House of Representatives. For the first time in American history, people outside the nation's capital could watch their government in action, without interruption and without editorial comment.

Since those early days of covering the House, C-SPAN has grown into a multifaceted entity. It is now a combination of networks that provides diverse public affairs programming 24 hours a day.

Today, the mission of C-SPAN remains unchanged. The network does not stand between the viewer and the events it covers. Its original and ongoing goal is for its public affairs programming to serve as a vehicle that allows viewers to judge for themselves, and to critically assess current issues. In addition to House proceedings, C-SPAN offers a front-row seat to other public affairs events from the nation's capital and across the country.

In 1986, the cable industry created C-SPAN 2 to cablecast live sessions of the U.S. Senate. C-SPAN 2's round-the-clock programming complements the original C-SPAN network by offering viewing alternatives to cable TV audiences interested in public affairs.

Editorial Review Board

Jane Blankenship
University of Massachusetts

George Grice
Radford University

John Sisco
Southwest Missouri State University

John Sullivan
University of Virginia

PRIVATELY FUNDED
TO SERVE THE PUBLIC
BY AMERICA'S CABLE
TELEVISION COMPANIES

C-SPAN

C-SPAN in the Communication Classroom:

Theory and Applications

Edited by
Janette Kenner Muir
George Mason University

Table of Contents

Part III Understanding Media

Part IV Crafting Research

■ 1
Discovering C-SPAN: An Introduction

Janette Kenner Muir

When I embarked on my journey to the University of Virginia as a visiting assistant professor a few years ago, I had no idea how much my life would be changed. It was not Mr. Jefferson's philosophy, nor the hallowed University halls that made such an impact. It was a wry, pipe-smoking, gray-headed professor who introduced me to the C-SPAN network and the rich programming it had to offer. Referring to himself as a "luddite" who barely knew how to work a remote control, let alone think about the process of editing tapes, this professor opened my eyes to a new way of thinking about the power of television, and its capacity to teach students critical thinking skills. Little did I know at the time how much C-SPAN would one day be a part of my teaching and scholarship. My introduction to C-SPAN that year was a valuable gift which I now take with me on my continuing journey.

The skeptic may wonder why anyone would be interested in using C-SPAN in the classroom. Aren't our syllabi already crowded with information we have to present during the semester? How could there possibly be time for showing tapes, analyzing programs and listening to full speeches? Isn't C-SPAN by its very nature just a series of talking heads which will bore students to sleep? What about all the time it takes to find something you want and edit it for the class?

All of these questions are important ones. Using videotape in the classroom is rarely easy, regardless of how skilled a person is. At many universities, mine included, instructors must track down a VCR and monitor, bring it to class, set it up, and then run the tape hoping that the segment cued with the counter at home somewhat matches the school's machine. Or the university may have out-dated or broken down audio-visual equipment known to chew tapes to shreds and spit them back to the bewildered instructor causing her to lose her most cherished segment of a House debate. It is not easy to be a modern day professor who in a moment's nod can push a button, flip a switch and provide instant video for a class.

Yet, there is something about television that really works for students. Many professors who use videotape in their classes will remark about the way interest is sparked when the television is brought to the classroom. I know from my own experience that students truly look forward to the days when I walk into class carrying a stack of videotapes. I never cease to be amazed how an entire class mood can suddenly shift when we turn to the television for an illustration. Students raised on this medium seem to easily learn from it; it provides a visual focal point for principles which might otherwise lay dormant in abstractions.

But why C-SPAN? What does it offer the student that another network or media form might not? The best way to explain its benefits is by providing some background about the network.

The C-SPAN Network

In 1979, after several years of groundwork laid by Brian Lamb, C-SPAN (the Cable-Satellite Public Affairs Network) was formed as a non-profit cooperative of the cable industry, dedicated to providing the public with gavel-to-gavel coverage of the House of Representatives. By 1982, the service was expanded to twenty-four hours, with continued commitment to the House, and expanded coverage to presidential addresses, National Press Club speeches, Congressional hearings and other noteworthy events happening around Washington, D.C. After the 1986 Senate vote to allow television cameras into its chamber, a second network was added, C-SPAN 2. Funding for these channels comes primarily from cable television sub-scribers and approximately three cents of every cable bill funds the network.

With this operating budget, C-SPAN maintains its commitment to the House and Senate, while at the same time covering White House speeches, rallies, international political forums such as the British and Canadian Houses of Parliament, the Japanese Diet, and the European Community. Recently we have seen segments of news from Moscow and London, on-the-spot coverage of the Persian Gulf war, and the complete Clarence Thomas/Anita Hill Hearings. As the 1992 political campaign unfolds, Americans follow the candidates through the various primary races, the conventions, and the general election. C-SPAN's Road to the White House series has been praised for its coverage of the candidates, its presentation of political commercials, and its philosophy to let voters decide what they believe to be important.

C-SPAN's goal is to provide "in-depth coverage of the American political system, its elected officials, and the journalists who cover it" (*C-SPAN Guide for Educators*, 2). Unlike conventional networks, C-SPAN does not edit events to make them interesting or entertaining, they are covered in their entirety, absent commentary and analysis (Lamb, 1988, xvi.). The philosophy is to let the viewers watch and decide for themselves their positions on various issues. The intent is to have cameras present, covering what happens absent the spin control and commentary which follows on other networks. Interviews with authors, journalists and politicians, round out the perspectives presented. While this can make for long, often tedious talk about issues, it also can provide illuminating moments about policy-making in action.

Following the philosophy of the network, the viewer call-in show plays a significant role by providing a vehicle for the public voice. Call-ins are dispersed throughout the weekly program, follow major political addresses or events, and often feature guests relevant to the issue of the day. For example, a political consultant might appear and discuss the merits of a particular campaign, a law professor might review the testimony of a Supreme Court nominee, or a representative might appear on a day when an important bill is being debated in the House. Following some discussion, the phone lines are opened for people to call the network, voice their opinions, ask questions, or clarify positions.

The focus for C-SPAN is primarily on the *process* of decision-making. By being in the right place at the right time, letting the cameras roll, and presenting unedited material to the public, C-SPAN provides a way for us to examine the machinations of politics, to see it in action with all its warts and all its beauty. By offering a vehicle for public expression, the network empowers people to watch, speak out and decide for themselves what they believe and value.

A Resource for Research and Teaching

As is evident from the above discussion, C-SPAN is dedicated to educating the public about issues and ideas. With this in mind, numerous services have been developed which can aid the educator who undertakes exploring the programming and using it for teaching and research.

C-SPAN in the Classroom

As a way to provide a direct link to educators throughout the country, C-SPAN developed a program known as *C-SPAN in the Classroom*. Headed by Linda Heller, Educational Services Director, this program provides educators at the secondary and college level with information about C-SPAN and how to use it in the classroom. Since its inception, the program has developed an educator's hotline with up-to-date programming information, a newsletter featuring instructional essays and information about educators, and seminars and workshops around the country. Three times a year C-SPAN sponsors a two-day seminar for educators to explain how the network operates and how it can be used in the classroom. Additionally, C-SPAN representatives will often be seen at major communication conventions conducting workshops, serving on panels, or running exhibition booths.

C-SPAN's liberal copyright policy is another feature of the network's commitment to educators. Educators and degree granting educational institutions are given the right to tape any C-SPAN program off the air without receiving direct permission from the network, provided taping is for school use. Instructors can tape programs, assign students to watch videos, or edit videotapes for their own classroom use. Tapes may be kept for as long as they are needed, and no fee is required (*C-SPAN in the Classroom: Teacher's Guide*, 1991, 1).

Any educator interested in the resources provided by C-SPAN can become a member of *C-SPAN in the Classroom* by registering with the network's education program. The membership is free and the educator will receive access to the hotline, the monthly newsletter, and numerous resources to enhance classroom teaching. Information about how to contact C-SPAN's educational service is included in the Appendix at the end of this book.

The Purdue Archives

The Purdue University Public Affairs Video Archives was created in 1987 as a cooperative venture between Purdue University and C-SPAN. Committed to providing a complete video record for education and research, the Archives now houses thousands of hours of C-SPAN programming, and produces duplicates of recordings for nominal fees. The Archives has also designed a program called the "Academic Consortium" which is available to institutions for reviewing tapes on a short-term loan basis.

All programming on both C-SPAN channels twenty-four hours per day, seven days per week is recorded by the Archives. A date, time and channel stamp is permanently placed on all tapes, and programming is indexed in the Archives computer system. Each program is entered with the following information: program category, description, date, place and sponsorship of the event, names, titles and affiliations of those who appear on the program (Browning, 1990, xiv). Identification numbers are provided for each program; you will see these referred to in this volume.

The Archives is fast becoming one of the largest public affairs collections in the country. Having outgrown their present facilities, they look forward to a new, permanent building, and new uses of technology to distribute information. Currently, data is provided in quarterly catalogues, and the Archives is exploring ways to permit on-line access to catalogues and to publish indexes on CD-ROM. The Archives provides an important resource for educators and scholars; contact information about this resource is included in the Appendix.

Suggestions for Using C-SPAN

Having used C-SPAN programming for several years now, I have learned by much trial and error. Below are some suggestions which may help to make your C-SPAN experience more rewarding.

Short Cuts for Off-Air Taping

As my friend at the University of Virginia occasionally reminds me, C-SPAN is not user friendly for those who want easily identifiable segments to illustrate important points. There are, however, some formats which are easier to work with. These formats are listed below in Eastern Standard Time.

Call-in Shows (Monday-Friday, 8:00 a.m. and 6:30 p.m.; also scheduled following major events). Usually the first part of the show clarifies information, and then the phone lines are opened to the public. This programming is frequently featured after major political speeches and events. For example, during the first week of the Persian Gulf war, phone lines were open around the clock for viewers to call in and express their concerns.

One Minute Speeches (daily when Congress is in session). Many representatives depend on the one minute speeches to present party messages, provide tributes to constituents, and argue about policy issues. They provide excellent models of short speeches, often illustrating simple mistakes people make while giving speeches.

Event of the Day (8:00 - 11:00 p.m. Monday-Friday). If Congress is in session, the event of the day may be preempted. However, this program generally covers important events aired during the day. The Educators Hot-line is useful for learning what events will be covered in this program.

Short Subjects (Mondays, 6:45 a.m.). Running approximately ten minutes, this program is primarily designed for high school teachers, although many will find the information presented valuable for introductory classes. A teacher's guide is available for this program.

Journalists Round Table (Friday 8:00 - 9:30 a.m., repeated on Saturday). This program features journalists reviewing the events of the week. Occasionally, clips from other shows will be highlighted.

Communications Today (Saturdays, 11:00 a.m.). This program focuses on media trends, technology, and communications law.

Supreme Court Review/America in the Courts (Saturdays). These programs cover issues dealing with the courts. Salient Supreme Court topics will frequently be discussed by legal scholars and journalists; judicial conferences, moot courts, and speeches by justices will often be featured.

National Press Club Speeches (Saturdays, 6:00 p.m.). C-SPAN covers all National Press Club luncheon speeches.

Booknotes (Sundays, 8:00 - 9:00 p.m.). A useful way to learn about a particular author, Booknotes features a variety of books and authors, some of which are useful to the educator. For example, I have used a segment from an interview with Peggy Noonan where she discusses her role in the Reagan Administration to illustrate some of the problems speech writers face in working with political leaders.

Question Time (Sundays, 9:00 - 9:30 p.m.). Question time in the British Parliament provides a wealth of information about English politics, from the decorum of address to the arguments used to advance positions.

This list is not exhaustive, but it does provide some general scheduling information which you may find useful.

Tracking Down Material

Beyond the programs listed above, there are some ways you might track down material. First, take advantage of the hot-line for up-to-date information. Calls made between 9:00 a.m. and 5:00 p.m. (EST, M-F) will reach a C-SPAN employee who can directly answer your questions. Calls made at other times will receive a lengthy recording about up-coming programs.

Second, throughout the day C-SPAN tries to update viewers about programming. An on-air program schedule is provided daily (See Appendix). It is also useful to remember that C-SPAN frequently re-airs important events on both channels.

If material is no longer available off the air, the next place to contact is the Purdue Archives. The staff is friendly and competent, and with very little information, can often track down exactly what you are looking for. The Archives also offers Videoguides to some tapes which provide detailed information as to what each tape contains.

Using a VCR

While this *is* the 1990s, the age of high tech computers and high definition television, many of us are, like my UVA friend, luddites when it comes to technology. With some time and perhaps a little bit of training, anyone can learn to master the VCR. Here are a few suggestions which might help the training process along.

Using Tape. While not a prerequisite for mastering the VCR, it has become apparent through the years that high quality tape, while higher in cost, is much better for longevity purposes. If you want your tape to last, make sure the quality is good. Before taping, it is useful to fast forward the tape to the end and then reverse back to the beginning. This will help to work out kinks within the videocassette which could result in distortion during the taping.

Tape While You View. I frequently leave a tape in my machine and let it run at night while I watch television. Usually, as I watch C-SPAN I will come across an interesting segment which might be useful for class. By taping through the evening I have gathered material to go through later. If there seems to be nothing useful, then I can just record over what I have taped.

Use Two VCRS. While many of us are at the stage of trying to just master one VCR, it is useful to at least consider the value of having two connected together. This may begin to sound too complicated, but with a little practice it is easy to edit between the two machines, and you can identify those segments which will be most relevant for your classes. Edited sections may look a little rough around the edges, but students still appreciate the effort. Having the capacity to edit will allow you to group various illustrative elements together on single tapes.

Getting Students Involved

Many of the authors in this text will explain ways to get students involved in skill development. Another aspect of student involvement, however, is using students for independent studies or special class sections to review tapes and produce guides for their use. This not only gives them experience in writing synopses, but can also teach them editing techniques.

Talk with Colleagues

One of the best ways to learn about what is on C-SPAN is by talking to others who watch and use the network. Those of us who are not "C-SPAN junkies" depend on information from others about useful programming. The educators' newsletter often shares interesting ideas and programs someone has used. By talking to each other about the programming, we can learn much more about what it has to offer. This sharing is, in large part, the philosophy that guides this project.

About the Book

For several years, the C-SPAN education program has been interested in exploring the possibility of a co-produced volume with the Speech Communication Association. This book represents the culmination of these labors. Those who study communication have much to gain from exploring C-SPAN. The purpose of this book is not to provide a gratuitous cheering section for the network. Indeed, as one begins to seriously explore the offerings, it is easy to be overwhelmed by the amount of effort it may take to create a usable piece of videotape for the classroom. The purpose, however, is to provide another teaching resource, by letting educators speak for themselves. Thirteen essays, of varying length, demonstrate the ways C-SPAN is being used for teaching and research. It is hard to mask the enthusiasm; many educators, as you will see, are clearly committed to this resource.

Following this introductory chapter, the book is divided into four major sections. The first part includes longer essays which primarily deal with the use of C-SPAN in empowering student awareness and action. Whillock's essay addresses the advantages C-SPAN holds for teaching critical thinking and perpetuating societal values. Smith explores how C-SPAN programming can be used in political communication classes to increase awareness about political symbols, language and ideology. The essay by Blankenship addresses the role of women in politics, using segments from C-SPAN to illustrate the construction of "political reality" and the "silencing" of women in the political arena. Muir considers the importance of C-SPAN programming in teaching students to think critically and respond effectively to environmental problems. By focusing on the development of citizenship skills, these authors argue that educators can use C-SPAN to empower student action.

The second section of this book includes shorter essays which directly focus on communication skill development. Hugenberg suggests that videotapes can be edited into short segments useful for illustrating elements of presentational speaking and delivery. Boileau discusses the use of the British Parliament's Question Time as a way to help students gain a better understanding of how parliamentary rules of procedure work within the formal setting. Neumann identifies how C-SPAN can be used in a persuasion course to help students learn to identify emotive language, nonverbal behavior, and demographic issues.

The next set of essays deals with understanding media issues, and using C-SPAN to teach journalism skills. The essay by Hadwiger and Paul discusses how focusing on the "primary event" of the week can enhance student understanding and appreciation for the network. Drushel incorporates C-SPAN into his Electronic Media policy course by examining panel discussions and conferences specific to this area of study. Snyder describes how C-SPAN programming can be used for students in journalism reporting classes. Finally, Carveth discusses ways that gatekeeping and agenda-setting can be illustrated, using the Hill/Thomas Hearings as a contemporary example.

The final section of this volume briefly explores a different aspect of C-SPAN use by looking at two contributions which address ways that C-SPAN can be used for research. Schnell offers an intercultural perspective by focusing on C-SPAN coverage of China and perceptions generated within the United States. Golden's essay considers the rhetorical style of James A. Traficant in his use of one minute speeches and call in shows on C-SPAN.

Together, these essays represent much time and energy spent in exploring and recognizing a wide variety of uses for C-SPAN. Each of the authors use C-SPAN in their classes, realize the benefits in its use, and continue to recruit other educators to the growing body of committed C-SPAN users. As a composite of energy devoted to understanding and using C-SPAN, the whole is much greater than the sum of its parts. Together these essays tell an important story about the impact C-SPAN has on educating our students. They have made an important contribution to the task of educating students for the twenty-first century.

There are others who have contributed to this book in substantial ways and should be acknowledged for their efforts. First, appreciation is extended to Jim Gaudino, Jim Chesebro, and the Speech Communication Association, for agreeing to co-sponsor this project with C-SPAN. This volume underscores the commitment SCA has to providing important resources for communication educators. Appreciation is also extended to Ann West and Helena Geipel who ensured that this manuscript maintains SCA's high standards of quality.

It is also important to recognize those who served on the editorial review board for this project: Jane Blankenship, George Grice, John Sisco, and John Sullivan. Material was returned in a timely fashion with thoughtful comments and suggestions for improvement. No editor could have asked for more, and their efforts in this endeavor are greatly appreciated.

There are others who played important roles in helping me track down references, proofread manuscripts, and enter data. Anne Davis, Star Muir, and Glenn Smith were significant in bringing this project to completion.

The staff at the Purdue University Archives was instrumental in providing identification numbers for the various tapes discussed in this volume.

Finally, there would not even be a volume of essays on C-SPAN were it not for Linda Heller, C-SPAN's Educational Services Director. This book, in many ways, is her vision. At the very least, it is a testament to all that she has taught us.

I will be forever grateful to my friend at the University of Virginia for introducing me to the C-SPAN network. Since that time I have met many dedicated scholars, and learned that we all struggle with how to be better teachers. I have watched those directly involved in the network and seen in them a true commitment to C-SPAN's philosophy. I have watched my students react to the lofty platitudes of a president or congressional leader, and I am convinced that they are indeed learning to think more critically. As a teacher, I believe that this is where our future must lie.

My friend gave me a wonderful gift. This volume is part of my effort to pass that gift along to you.

References

Browning, R. X (1990). About the public affairs video archives. *Public affairs video archives, 1989, no. 2.* West Lafayette, IN: Purdue Research Foundation.

C-SPAN in the classroom: an educator's guide (1988). Washington DC: The National Cable Satellite Corporation.

C-SPAN in the classroom: a teacher's guide (1991). Washington, DC: The National Cable Satellite Corporation.

Lamb, B., et al. (1989). *C-SPAN: America's town hall.* Washington, DC: Acropolis Books Ltd.

Sullivan, J. (1990). Short cuts to short clips. An unpublished guide to C-SPAN programming.

☐ Part I

Empowering Student Thought and Action

■ 2

Ideology and Implications of Media Use

Rita Whillock

This essay examines the ideological implications of using C-SPAN as a teaching vehicle, and argues that C-SPAN does more than enhance teaching. It also results in the perpetuation of certain educational and societal values. The ways C-SPAN enhances classroom instruction are explored, including the use of the network as a critical tool, and the way it explicates the decision-making process.

Anyone who has had the privilege of attending the "C-SPAN in the Classroom" seminar may remember the opening remarks of Education Director Linda Heller. In her statement, she reminds the group of academics that C-SPAN is a tool. The seminar is not designed to indoctrinate professors but to invigorate them through interaction with their colleagues about ways to become more effective in the classroom. That is the expressed purpose of the conference. Yet after you attend the seminar or talk with the many professors who routinely use C-SPAN, you become aware that there is an ideology implied by the use of this tool.

This essay examines the ideological implications of using C-SPAN as a teaching vehicle. I argue that the use of C-SPAN does more than enhance teaching, although that is certainly an advantage. It also results in the perpetuation of certain educational and societal values. Consideration of these premises is critical in order to discover the reason that there are so many believers in C-SPAN as a teaching tool.

Enhancing Classroom Instruction

For many in the profession, training in innovative teaching methods is not a requisite part of their degree plan. Yet upon graduation, they are propelled into a classroom setting. Many, if not most, eventually develop the skills necessary to teach, but there is also a great "silent" majority who probably admit that they are not as dynamic as they secretly wish they were.

For the last decade or so, there has been an implied belief that video aids would somehow help make better teachers. In an attempt to encourage the use of video technology, universities routinely provide professors access to VCR hook-ups. Yet even though universities espouse a commitment to teaching excellence, they rarely provide professors opportunities to learn effective teaching techniques from each other, nor do they assist professors in learning how to best adapt technology to suit their purposes. As a result, the use of video as a teaching aid is astonishingly ineffectual. In canned (or prepackaged) videotaped presentations, the professor has little control over the objectives, presentation of ideas, or the content. In essence, the video becomes the teacher, the professor merely a commentator. These stock "training" films also typically possess a negative reputation among students. One reason is that the materials presented are not very engaging. Perhaps it is because the purpose of a video is often ill defined. Additionally, most have generic purposes in order to appeal to a wide spectrum of uses and thereby increase sales potential. Students and professors alike argue that as a result these videos are not fully germane to the topic at hand. Similarly, complaints include that they are quickly dated, rarely cover timely events, and provoke little meritorious conversation.

The educational outreach program of C-SPAN attempts to constructively address these issues. First, C-SPAN is committed to helping professors become better teachers. By providing the "C-SPAN in the Classroom" seminar, as well as a host of outreach programs at national conventions, C-SPAN's educational unit demonstrates an active concern about what goes on in the classroom. Yet unlike some who gripe about quality teaching and do little about it, C-SPAN offers professors resources, namely other professors who have successfully integrated these materials into their classes. They also assist in identifying techniques that can be used to achieve demonstrable results. This book is a testament to that effort.

Second, C-SPAN provides opportunities for professors to learn how to effectively adapt video materials to meet their teaching objectives. Yet they do not presuppose what a teacher's needs may be. Therefore, C-SPAN does not prepackage or control the footage being viewed. Instead, the network offers insight into how materials might be adapted to suit specific purposes. The professor is in complete control of the material chosen and the ways to make video footage relevant to a particular discussion.

The motives for C-SPAN's involvement with and commitment to improved classroom communication are not without benefit for both parties. Educators learn to become more effective. At the same time, when professors use C-SPAN they get a refresher course in civics. These lessons are passed along to their students. By utilizing examples from the everyday practice of government, students are provided an incentive to become better informed. In order to participate in discussions, students must actively analyze the events they are witnessing.

Teaching Critical Thinking

When students are taught to analyze the form, content and procedural packaging of information, they are learning not to remain passive receptors of information (e.g. Kubey & Csikszentmihalyi, 1990). They are being taught instead to critically analyze data through the events unfolding before them. Crucially, they are learning ways to prevent their own manipulation.

These are not just moral issues, though that justification alone should merit analysis. At stake is the ability (some might prefer the word *freedom*) to make choices about our future. Without an understanding in the art of persuasion and the process of governing, the only ones who will find these tools worthy are those elite who might prefer the masses to be ignorant of their utility.

There is a decided need to teach students to identify manipulative tactics and expose them for what they are. This position was eloquently argued by Aristotle in *The Rhetoric*. Without such protection, he contended, the masses will become even more susceptible to rhetorical coercion. This is not to argue that the public is routinely exploited, but that learning preventative strategies might preclude such an occurrence.

Learning how to thwart manipulative practices is not the only necessary defense. Equally important is that students learn to reduce the climate of opinion in which manipulative tactics can flourish. Reducing information distortion is one way to accomplish that end.

Most citizens are aware that the news they watch provides only an impression of the actual proceedings. At best, the stories form one part of the whole picture from which the news story emerged. Without being cynical, the public correctly perceives that this also reduces their abilities to make good decisions. Written news accounts are dependent upon the interpretation of the reporter. News stories covered via radio and television, while providing a window for citizens to witness events themselves, are inadequate for giving a full accounting of the events. This is heightened by the awareness that most of these stories are thirty to sixty seconds in length. The brevity of coverage is suitable for providing impressions of a news event, but insufficient for providing any detailed information. By featuring a full, unedited record of events, C-SPAN responds to the information distortion brief accountings of events inherently produce.

Information distortion is not only a result of the brevity of most news accounts; it is also created by the paucity of information sources. Another reason people might suspect they could be manipulated is because their choices of information are, in fact, limited. Despite American commitment to free press and free speech, sources of information are becoming more and more restricted. In all, less than three percent of cities in the United States which have a newspaper have more than one (Facts, 1988). As a result, the detailed information concerning issues of community welfare are increasingly channeled through one print source. Television news faces similar problems. Instead of competitive reporting, programs often key off the headline stories of rival news agencies. As in the alleged affair between Presidential candidate Bill Clinton and an Arkansas state employee, Americans witnessed the network news giants keying off the headlines of an ethically suspicious publication for one of its major news stories. The current lack of news competition has aided in the creation of a climate of public distrust (see Postman, 1985; Wicklein, 1981). Without disparate voices challenging ideas and assumptions, people are aware that they may not get all the information they need to render an impartial opinion of events. This is the news equivalent of a jury being forced to render a verdict without benefit of hearing an adequate defense.

The climate is further nurtured by the fact that the news hole in most every commercial news venture is dramatically shrinking in favor of advertising (*Advertising Age*, 1990). This limits the amount of information presented. Studies of political campaigns amply demonstrate the result of these actions with regard to the scarcity of information the public receives about the people they would elect to the nation's highest office. Except for the advertisements the campaigns pay for themselves, political candidates running for president in 1988 had less than ten seconds to make their case on the evening news (Cunningham, 1990). This is hardly sufficient time to reply to the complex issues that may arise during the course of a campaign. The result is a string of sound bites. Such "media speak" may provide a sense of the news, but is inadequate for the dialectic needs of an informed citizenry.

The impact of these news trends is noteworthy. Obviously, these actions serve to constrict the flow of information. As the news hole and competition for detailed analysis decreases, less information is conveyed through the medium.

There are alternative sources for finding more complete information about newsworthy events. The *Congressional Record*, for example, is available in many libraries. Yet despite the fact that the public has alternative means of seeking out information, those sources are not as easily accessible as traditional news channels. In this information age, ease of access is often as important to consumers as the information itself.

Additionally, consumers are finding it increasingly difficult to find original source information. While that may have always been true, to a certain extent the effects of this lack of access were mollified through competitive news reporting. Without a healthy competition of ideas, viewers will become reliant on the interpretation given events by the one reporter assigned to cover a story or on the media pool report.

C-SPAN is not a salve for all these ills but it is a viable start. Although it does not attempt to cover all types of news events, it does provide a readily accessible, complete accounting of national debates in U.S. House and Senate proceedings. Their gavel-to-gavel coverage of these sessions eliminates the necessity to rely on news interpretations or wait for the *Congressional Record* to be shipped from the Government Printing Office. Whether the public has learned to use C-SPAN yet or not, access to information without commentary is now available.

Further, by using C-SPAN as a reference tool, professors can effectively teach students the problems, opportunities and strategies at work in news creation. Students, for example, can watch an event like David Duke's speech before the Ford Hall Forum or the testimony of witnesses before a Congressional committee like that of Oprah Winfrey on child abuse, then write headlines or a two-minute news story summarizing the event before comparing their interpretation to that of the newscasters on the evening news. Questions can be argued in class concerning which video clips should accompany the story, how much of the story should be reporter narrative and how much should use direct testimony. Coverage of the event by each the major channels can be compared. *Critically,* questions of interpretation can be debated by going back to the original source material presented in full context. By completing this exercise, students can determine for themselves what levels of bias exist in the presentation of the news or which news outlets are most credible to them by virtue of how closely the reports resemble their own interpretation of events. Students can also begin to grasp the persuasive strategies used to further certain interests. During election years, C-SPAN coverage is particularly useful in teaching these lessons. Programs often feature strategists and consultants openly discussing what steps a campaign will take in order to counter an opposing candidate. Students can then compare the strategy statements with the commercials, news coverage, and other visible manifestations of the campaign. They can debate the soundness of the strategy itself; they can estimate the perceived effectiveness of the strategy once executed; and they can evaluate the quality of performance used to operationalize that strategy.

C-SPAN cannot teach students how to wade through the host of information it broadcasts in order to reach good decisions. That is the job of parents and educators. But by using C-SPAN, we can provide accurate and vivid examples of what is heard, and what is not, how information is packaged, and how it is compressed into headlines.

Providing Diverse Information Sources

In the television industry, audience ratings often guide what shows will be produced, what types of issues will be addressed at length, and who will serve as the spokesperson. Person-on-the-street interviews are mostly the result of happenstance, rather than because a citizen has a thoughtful opinion of an issue being addressed. And, except for a few talk shows, television provides little opportunity for viewers to become participants in the events they witness. C-SPAN is the exception.

C-SPAN opens the air waves to viewers on a regular basis. In fact, the network invites participation by making it a part of its standard schedule. The advantage of the viewer call in segment is not just that interested people get an opportunity to voice their opinions in a national forum. Callers are also able to express positions that might be suppressed though traditional news outlets. Call in segments are not prescreened so that only the most interesting and stimulating are aired. The network does not concern itself with whether a viewer's opinion is popular or not. As a result, C-SPAN's national forums enrich our understanding of the perceptions held by the many diverse and often competing factions of society. Yet this is not the only way C-SPAN promotes national debate.

When Congress is not in session, C-SPAN offers a variety of news and information shows. Viewers may be invited to listen and interact with defendants of flag-burning, advocates of drug legalization, or critics of the

"Star Wars" defense system. Or C-SPAN may cover the proceedings of some special interest group meeting in the Washington corridor.

C-SPAN likes to think of itself as America's "Town Hall." Producers work to provide a forum that permits viewers to come together to consider national issues. Simultaneously, some groups choose to meet in the Washington area specifically because they hope to get national coverage for their issues through the C-SPAN forum. In essence, C-SPAN is attempting to be a forum for national citizen debate.

Fortunately, C-SPAN also recognizes that the United States does not function in isolation from other nations. Perhaps as a result of the shrinking news hole, perhaps a function of decreased travel budgets in difficult economic times, or because of a lack of intercultural understanding, many people find it increasingly difficult to explore a "world view" through American news coverage of events. Students travelling abroad are often shocked at how Americans are viewed and the discrepant interpretations they have of world events. Even when international events are covered, many critics note that the news is still covered by American reporters and tailored to suit traditional news formats. Even news wires demand style and formula writing. Indeed, critics have long argued for the need for a more global, less myopic perspective of the world.

CNN's worldwide coverage has worked to rectify this imbalance at least in the arena of international government (see Wittemore, 1990). Yet the news is still covered by American reporters and tailored to suit traditional news formats.

C-SPAN has helped to address this issue through coverage of the proceedings in the House of Commons in Great Britain and those of the Canadian Parliament. In recent years, C-SPAN has developed additional educational programs concerning international arenas such as the European Economic Community, the Pacific Rim, and the United Nations.

Through such debates and discussions, viewers get a sense of how others may view world events as well as the concerns, interests, and evaluations of other parties concerned. At the same time, watchers can begin to understand something of the climate in which decisions are made as well as something of another culture's customs and procedures. In United Nations debates, viewers have the unique opportunity to see how different cultures interact with one another, as well as the problems inherent in negotiating across cultural differences.

Importantly, C-SPAN does not package these events to suit the tastes of American audiences. As in the gavel-to-gavel coverage of Congress, viewers are only provided a window through which to view events as they naturally occur. Producers stay out of the business of interpreting the meaning or significance of these events.

Without understanding how others think and how they come to certain conclusions, Americans will have little understanding for the values of other people and insufficient empathy for their perspective of world events. Much to C-SPAN's credit, the network aided in reducing the Cold War barriers between the U.S. and its former enemy, the U.S.S.R. For the first time, American audiences are able to watch the Moscow evening news report. By doing so, C-SPAN provides an access point for understanding the problems and challenges faced as a nation undergoes a drastic revolution in its form of government. Without a news filter, C-SPAN permits us to explore the struggles our former adversaries now face. Its coverage helps attune us to their problems. Equally important, it permits us to hear their point of view in their own words, spoken in their own way.

Evaluating the Decision-Making Process

Whether exploring diverse cultures or disparate voices within our own society, much is to be learned by observing the decision-making process itself. Current news practices provide a false prism of decision-making and governing processes. The "highlights" of today's news as seen on the evening broadcasts typically focus on outcomes, not processes. As a result, viewers are not aware of the complex issues that surround a decision, how arguments are couched or the evidence the rhetors judge important.

Put simply, students are not being trained to fathom the complexity of decision-making processes. Many students have little understanding of how a bill becomes a law, how the committee structure works in Congress, or the procedures and protocols that influence debate. Even many of those who learned these civic lessons have never seen Congress in action. In an age of quick-fix solutions, students are better served by understanding these intricacies than by succumbing to the myth that outcomes are the only way to judge the moral and ethical dimensions of government. C-SPAN does not assume that processes are learned only by observation. Throughout the year, the network airs Short Subject programs designed to assist viewers in understanding the process issues. Segments for the 1991-92 school year included informational programs on the "First Amendment," the "Powers and Duties of the President," "Congressional Redistricting," the "Library of Congress," "The Supreme Court," "Senate Leadership," as well as a host of others.

If it is true that experience is the best teacher, what better way to learn how the process works than by witnessing an event first hand? Once the process has been explained, professors can use C-SPAN's coverage of committee work, for example, to illustrate the theory as put into operation.

Perhaps as important as the procedural lessons professors can teach is the habit of mind students need to develop as good decision-makers and citizens. Many of them would never think to monitor C-SPAN coverage of events as a means of evaluating the decision-making process. Yet C-SPAN is available in more than 40 million households through local cable systems. This is a readily accessible, easy-to-use medium. The challenge is to get students to think about the network as an information tool. Some will become C-SPAN junkies, but most will learn to use C-SPAN as they would any other tool, when it is appropriate and when it is important to them. This is just one way they can learn to routinely check on the reliability of news information and get more in-depth information on issues of personal importance.

Conclusions

The use of C-SPAN as a teaching tool has direct significance for the way we teach as well as the lessons we implicitly pass along to our students. If we are to use this tool appropriately and to its full potential, we must consider these implications.

C-SPAN does not purport to be a news channel per se. Its job is not to provide sound bites of news events or interpret their significance. It does, however, provide a means of teaching students about the events that make news. Moreover, it demonstrates the depth of discourse that accompanies decisions on matters of state. A steady diet of even a portion of the network's coverage would undoubtedly result in a better informed citizenry. This volume of articles and classroom exercises on the use of C-SPAN is an invaluable tool to professors concerned with making lectures and class discussions timely and relevant. C-SPAN is an appropriate vehicle through which our lessons can be explicated and enlivened. Moreover, C-SPAN is a way of teaching students about the way we practice and operationalize our societal values. As such, it deserves our support and attention.

References

Are there more ads now? (1990, July 2). *Advertising Age*, p. 19.

Cunningham, C. (1990). Smoke and mirrors. *Campaign Magazine, 4*, 16-17.

Facts about newspapers (1988). Reston, VA: American Newspaper Publishers Association.

Kubey, R., and Csikszentmihalyi, M. (1990). *Television and the quality of life: How viewing shapes everyday experience.* Hillsdale, NJ: Lawrence Erlbaum.

Postman, N. (1985). *Amusing ourselves to death: Public discourse in the age of show business.* New York: Viking.

Wicklein, J. (1981). *The electronic nightmare: The new communications and freedom.* New York: Viking.

Wittemore, H. (1990). *CNN: The inside story.* New York: Little, Brown.

■ 3

The Interpretive Systems Approach to Teaching Political Communication

Craig Allen Smith

This chapter summarizes the interpretive systems approach to teaching political communication and suggests four exercises that use it. An intrapersonal needs analysis of the 1988 Reagan, Bush, and Dukakis convention messages illuminates the relationship between needs and power. The symbols and language used by 1988 candidates Jack Kemp and Bruce Babbitt suggest the complexities of political symbolizing and language. A debate exchange between Bill Clinton and Jerry Brown invites consideration of the viewer's tendency to prefer one explanation over another and suggests the role of ideological rationalization. Finally, a panel on the film JFK provides opportunities to compare and contrast modes of reasoning that culminate in political logics.

At least since Aristotle's day, students of communication and rhetoric have been intrigued by the relationship between communication and politics. But 1991 will be remembered as a watershed year in the study of political communication because of three significant developments: the Speech Communication Association launched its Political Communication Division, the American Political Science Association's Political Communication Division held its first programs, and the Political Communication Divisions of the International Communication Association and the American Political Science Association announced plans for the new journal *Political Communication*.

Some members of these associations continue to regard political communication divisions as little more than additional theaters for the presentation of research in public address, mass communication, freedom of speech, public relations, and American studies. That criticism should not be dismissed without reflection. Indeed, students of political communication need to adopt parameters as well as core principles that define our field, and those are important functions of theory. We therefore need theories or models concerned primarily with political communication. Such models must emphasize both the political and the communicative properties, and they must frame the panoply of interests that have brought us together.

The author has advanced one such approach, an "Interpretive Systems" model, in an introductory political communication textbook (Smith, 1990), in a master syllabus (Smith, forthcoming), and forthcoming in a book on presidential leadership. This chapter suggests ways in which C-SPAN materials can be used to teach political communication courses from this interpretive systems perspective.

The Interpretive Systems Approach to Political Communication

The interpretive systems approach combines principles of General Systems Theory, symbolic interactionism, constructivism, schema theory, and symbolic convergence. Briefly, it holds that:

1) Each of us understands the world through our personal interpretive processes, which include motivating, symbolizing, preferencing, and reasoning.
2) Our appraisals of the world lead us toward relationships with others. Among these relationships are political communities built around social interpretive structures. These social structures evolve as a result of the following: shared motivating processes produce power, shared symbolizing produces language, shared preferencing produces ideology, and shared reasoning produces logic.
3) Each political community struggles for the right to define the world for others, such that temporarily dominant groups define and distribute the resources and sanctions.
4) Clues to the evolutionary political processes, their communities, and their progress can be found in political messages and in the differential reactions of audiences (Smith, 1990, pp. vii-ix).

The evolutionary interdependence of personal processes and negotiated social structures is central to the model. Individual humans have four innate and interdependent intrapersonal processes: we need, we symbolize, we prefer, and we reason. Because we never stop needing, symbolizing, preferring or reasoning—and because we are interested in the ways that people constitute and reconstitute their personal inventories of needs, symbols, preferences, and reasons—I have chosen to label these intrapersonal processes *motivating, symbolizing, preferencing,* and *reasoning.*

As individuals encounter one another they seek coordination by negotiating social interpretive structures. Their patterns of symbolizing when shared become their "language," their patterns of reasoning when shared become their "logic," and their patterns of preferencing when shared become their "ideology." Informal languages, logics, and ideologies can become formal Languages, Logics, and Ideologies if they are codified and published. Both formal or informal modes encourage the emergence of official mindguards and informal vigilantes who identify and chastise those who deviate from the accepted language, ideology, and logic.

Motives and needs can be congruent, compatible, complementary, or incompatible. In a social system the essence of "power" exists in the capacity to fulfill or to frustrate the needs of others, a capacity that often entails the obfuscation, camouflaging, or subordination of one's own needs. Bosmajian's (1983) *The Language of Oppression* demonstrates how the language of one interpretive community can disadvantage members of other communities. Governmental systems institutionalize these abilities to fulfill and frustrate needs in formal Powers, and much political communication concerns the legitimacy, the dispersal, and the propriety of those powers and their use.

Each interpretive structure defines the culture of an interpretive community, and political discourse occurs within and between these interpretive communities. Bormann's (1972, 1985) symbolic convergence theory shows how rhetorical fantasies chain out to create communities, and any framework for rhetorical criticism can be used to help students appreciate the spectrum of critical approaches. They can see, for example, that neo-Aristotelian studies reflect an established logic and that other communities' logics, such as feminist criticism, can often provide important comparative insights.

The interpretive communities' model also enables students to see how political advocates attempt to win and retain power by forging coalitions around, for instance, the preference of one community depicted in the language of another and justified using the logic of yet a third community. The 1947 "Truman Doctrine" blended the desire for a peaceful, friendly world with the familiar demonic symbolism of Nazism/Communism and the diplomatic logic of power balances. Democratic convention keynote addresses are useful examples of speakers trying to unify their disparate communities into a transcendent party, while sharply differentiating it from the Republican interpretive community.

In short, the approach helps students to see that political controversies arise because incongruent communities have conflicting interpretations of reality, each of which makes sense when viewed in terms of its own interpretive structure. Moreover, students begin to understand that these interpretive structures are created and learned only through communication.

Let us turn now to four class exercises that use the interpretive system approach. Each of these exercises can be used over a series of class periods or, after some fairly ambitious out-of-class tape editing, in a single class. Perhaps the level of the class should guide the level of the exercise: lower division students can view and respond rather superficially, whereas advanced or graduate students can write analytical papers.

Exercise One:
The Motivating Process and Political Empowerment

During the summer of 1988, George Bush and Michael Dukakis prepared to fill the shoes of Ronald Reagan, the most popular outgoing president in American history, always more popular than his political positions. What citizen needs did President Reagan fulfill? What citizen needs did Bush and Dukakis strive to meet in their efforts to replace? Finally, did Bush and Dukakis strive to meet similar or divergent needs?

The three tapes necessary for this exercise are all from the 1988 national conventions: the Reagan campaign film (ID# 3813), the Dukakis acceptance address (ID# 5725), and the Bush acceptance address (ID# 3848). Provide the class with a coding sheet handout that has in the leftmost column Maslow's hierarchy of needs (defined) on one side and Schutz's FIRO-B inventory (defined) on the other; with empty columns labelled Reagan, Dukakis, Bush, and total. Direct half the class to use the Maslow typology and half to use FIRO. It may be useful, as discussed below, for the students to note their salient demographic characteristics such as gender, race, party identification, ideological tendencies, level of political interest, education, religion, and so forth.

Instruct the class to ignore their preconceived impressions of the speakers, their parties, and their programs because they are interested in these documents as psychological gratifications, from which they could be easily distracted by partisan or ideological considerations. Instruct them, secondly, to follow the tape closely and to put a tally mark on their coding sheet every time that they hear or see something that speaks to one of *their own* psychological needs. Take the time necessary to discuss the task, possibly using a brief tape of something else for a dry run. Then have them watch the tapes in any order, either in class or at a campus viewing facility. Have them calculate the totals, across and down, to complete their tables.

The exercise can be completed in several different ways. Small classes can compare and contrast the need structures of the three documents. Did the two Republican documents provide a bridge from Reagan to Bush on the basis of psychological needs, or did Bush attempt to satisfy different needs? Did Dukakis offer psychological gratifications more like those of Reagan or Bush, or was his approach sufficiently different to suggest unique psychological needs among Democrats and Republicans? Did the sheer number of need appeals appear to be more important for any one document?

Large classes with computer facilities and trained graduate assistants can analyze the data using crosstabs, analysis of variance, and factor analysis. The results facilitate more precise discussions of empirical research, the significance of differences within and between groups, and the need factors along which these politicians' psychological gratifications load.

Whichever initial path is chosen, discussion should eventually turn to the students' own needs. Did clusters of students find different gratification patterns? The factor analysis may reveal clusters of students with similar gratifications.

The exercise should help the class to see (1) that individuals have idiosyncratic needs, (2) that politicians address their citizens' psychological needs, (3) that different rhetorical acts provide different psychological gratifications, (4) that people with similar motives will have a common basis for preferring a candidate, and (5) that a politician who seeks to gratify new needs risks alienating the people with the old needs.

What can we now observe about the transformation of these needs into informal power and formal political Power? Each of these messages (1) explicitly or implicitly addresses (2) the legitimacy and illegitimacy of needs that have been (3) fulfilled or frustrated. Ask students to tackle the following questions:

1) What legitimate needs does Reagan claim to have fulfilled?
2) What illegitimate needs does Reagan claim to have frustrated?
3) What legitimate needs does Reagan concede to have frustrated?
4) What illegitimate needs does Reagan admit to having fulfilled?

Replicate the exercise for Bush and Dukakis, asking which needs have been or will be frustrated and fulfilled. Ask the students armed with these profiles to analyze the needs that have been empowered and disenfranchised by Reagan, and those that Bush and Dukakis, respectively, promised to empower and disempower.

Exercise Two:
Symbolizing and Language in New Hampshire

If there were a Hall of Fame for communication cliches, the first to be enshrined would have to be, "Meanings are in people, not in words." Another way of stating that tidy aphorism is, "Meanings are among persons, not in words." The difference, of course, is that the restatement emphasizes that "people" is an aggregate of individuals, that the ultimate ascertainment of meaning is intensely personal, and that words are the links among individuals. Before one can be concerned about widely shared political language, then, we must attend to personal symbolizing. Do individual citizens possess the symbolic categories necessary to understand the political messages they hear? What happens when politicians employ words that are either too complex or to simple for voters? Finally, can symbolic complexity and simplicity become the foundation for political support?

Jack Kemp and Bruce Babbitt conducted unsuccessful campaigns for the presidency in 1988. The materials needed for this exercise are Kemp's press conference upon his arrival in New Hampshire after the first-tier Iowa caucuses (ID# 3674), Bruce Babbitt's remarks at the Tin Palace Restaurant in Durham, New Hampshire (ID# 1454), and the transcripts for each.

Students should be familiarized with the general nature of "personal construct systems" (Delia, O'Keefe, and O'Keefe, 1982; Smith, 1990, pp. 10-12). Especially relevant are the three dimensions of "differentiation" (the number of personal constructs), "articulation" (the degree of sophistication which those constructs are refined or usefully abstract), and "integration" (the manner in which the available constructs are connected to one another).

The students should then watch either Kemp or Babbitt with transcript in hand, preparing to answer the question: "What is this man talking about?" Discussion can pursue several paths: What constructs define the speaker's symbolic world? Is his world highly differentiated or undifferentiated? How are these constructs linked or integrated? Which are well-developed and articulated?

Kemp's press conference followed his disappointing showing in Iowa and he came out of the huddle with the intensity of a quarterback in the two-minute offense. Unfortunately, he was both flustered and oblivious to the fact that New Hampshire voters were not yet prepared for his complex message. It may not be an exaggeration to say that Kemp's remarks confused many of his supporters. After examining his remarks, students can work individually or in groups to translate Kemp's remarks for an audience of reasonably intelligent but previously uninformed voters. But empirical persuasion research has found that intelligent, highly educated, and high self-esteem individuals can be disproportionately persuaded by messages that seem to appeal to their intelligence, education, and general superiority. Could it be that Kemp's symbolic complexity was an important foundation of his support among campus Republicans, for whom support for Kemp functioned as a badge of intelligence education and symbolic complexity needed to understand his message?

It is difficult to conceive of an adult who would regard Babbitt's remarks at the Tin Palace as cognitively challenging. The former governor of Arizona drones on about the familiar, and drapes platitudes about like crepe paper. Students often laugh at his slow, monotonous, and self-important delivery, sometimes urging us to stop the tape. Especially interesting is Babbitt's coupling of a denunciation of the "old politics" of nostalgia with a long narrative about, and recitation from, the Kennedy inaugural. Do Babbitt's remarks convey or conceal his plans for presidential leadership? Do his words reveal the workings of his mind, or is he attempting to reach Reagan Democrats with the very nostalgia, platitudes, and popular myths that he condemns?

Neither Kemp nor Babbitt came close to winning his party's nomination. Can that be attributed, even in part, to their uses of language? Were there sufficient people out there speaking Kemp's language to win nomination and election? Indeed, were there people out there willing to learn Kemp's language? Did Babbitt discern the contradiction between his theme and his language? Have students rewrite Babbitt's remarks to enhance their meaningfulness to ordinary voters. Having done so, the class can debate whether their rewriting of Babbitt's remarks enhanced or undermined "good" political communication.

Exercise Three:
Preferencing and Refutation in Debates

"Preferencing" refers to the process of establishing personal priorities among one's psychological needs, beliefs, reasons and behaviors. Voting requires us not to rate candidates on a ten-point scale but to prefer one of the available alternatives. Leaders and citizens frequently must prefer either war or an unpalatable peace, inflation or unemployment, an important program or deficit reduction, conformity, or independence. At its most basic and inescapable level, preferencing is the process through which we prefer one advocate's account over another's.

A brief exchange during a 1992 Democratic candidates forum in Maryland (ID# 24738) provides an example of preferencing. Arkansas Governor Bill Clinton was regarded as the national frontrunner in the race for the Democratic nomination, but Paul Tsongas, Tom Harkin, and Jerry Brown all hoped to derail Clinton in Maryland. Late in the debate Brown attacked Clinton's environmental record in Arkansas as the worst in the nation. He read from newspaper articles and then passed them to Clinton. Harkin joined Brown in the attack on Clinton. Then Clinton responded to each of the articles with a specificity and confidence that suggested accuracy, while Harkin and Brown persisted in their claim that environmental groups had denounced Clinton's record.

Ask students anonymously to explain—in writing—who they believed and who they disbelieved, and their reasons for preferring that candidate's account. Ask them also to rate each candidate's statement on a scale of 0 (totally unbelievable) to 10 (totally believable). Then have the students trade papers and analyze each other's preferencing:

1) What reasons did students provide for believing Brown? Frequent answers include his environmental record, his references to independent watchdog groups, and the McCarthy-like article waving.
2) What reasons did students provide for disbelieving Brown? Frequent reasons include Brown's image as an eccentric, his wide-eyed intensity, and his inability to extend his initial claim.
3) What reasons did students provide for believing Clinton? Frequent answers include his indignation and his use of specifics.
4) What reasons did students provide for disbelieving Clinton? The most common answer is usually his "slickness."

Discussion of these first four questions can progress to higher levels:

1) How many students emphasized logical proof, and did they appear to weigh carefully competing claims, evidence, and connecting warrants?
2) How many students emphasized aspects of candidate style and persona?
3) How many students emphasized *both* logical and stylistic factors?
4) How many students were unable to articulate meaningfully either logical or stylistic factors ("I just think he was telling the truth.")?

Finally, when each student has categorized the written explanation into one of the latter four categories, calculate the Brown and Clinton scores for each category. If time permits, have students break into small groups to discuss their impressions. With more luck than planning you will have people with similar preferencing styles who prefer dissimilar candidates, students with dissimilar preferencing styles who prefer the same candidate, and the two predictable groups. Discussion tends to illustrate that preferencing often precedes careful reasoning. Many students prefer one person's account and rather transparently rationalize it.

To the extent that people with similar preferencing patterns join together and use those preferencing patterns as a reasoning shortcut, they may be said to share an ideology. This is a useful point at which to help students differentiate between ideologies (the shared preferences) that can be preferred for a variety of reasons, and ideologues (people who need ideological frameworks to understand politics) who move from one ideology to another with surprising ease.

Exercise Four: Reasoning

"Reasoning" is one's personal process for arranging symbols, preferences, and motives into a personally meaningful conception of reality. It is the process, literally, of "making sense" out of otherwise random stimuli. Any citizen who would avoid cognitive and affective inconsistency must find narratives that provide coherence for an array of needs, preferences, and symbols that otherwise conflict.

Although one can teach political reasoning in terms of syllogisms and enthymemes, it is generally more fruitful to emphasize narrative reasoning. Walter Fisher (1987) provides a narrative paradigm that encourages us to examine the ways in which narratives integrate philosophy, reason, and action. The narrative organizes the narrator's needs, symbols, and preferences to achieve both *narrative fidelity* and *narrative coherence*.

Narrative coherence refers to the ways in which the narrative satisfies our expectations of "good stories." These consist of (1) argumentative or structural coherence, (2) material coherence, and (3) characterological coherence. Narrative fidelity refers to the ways in which the story presents "accurate assertions about social reality and thereby constitutes good reasons for belief and action" (Fisher, 1987, p. 105). Essentially, good reasons are those that are tied to values, such that they enable one to prefer a course of action or an explanation on the basis of one's values. A narrator who offers a compelling story that articulates listener experiences and values will be the more persuasive.

The right-wing John Birch Society encountered a belief-dilemma in 1966 when President Johnson's war in Vietnam (which Birchers perceived as a Communist plot to destroy our economy) was opposed by campus demonstrators (whom the Birchers viewed as Communist agitators). One might have expected an exodus of members in search of a coherent narrative. Instead, they turned to their leader, Robert Welch, who explained that the Communist-infiltrated government, the Communist agitators and, for that matter, the leftist media, were all engaged in a spectacle of apparent conflict that actually proved (1) the cleverness of the Communists, (2) the extent to which Communism had taken over America, and (3) the importance of joining the Birch Society, lest one be duped by the conspirators. Welch's narrative built upon his followers' psychological hunger for authoritative explanations and their fundamental belief that a gigantic international conspiracy was afoot. Members faced with a choice between doubting their leader and their ideology on the one hand, and affirming and extending their faith in the leader and his ideological prophesies found solace in his narrative.

The grandfather of all examples of narrative rationality must be the Warren Commission report on the assassination of President John F. Kennedy. The Commission's conclusions have been debated for twenty-five years and several explanations have acquired adherents. The 1991 release of Oliver Stone's *JFK* marked a turning point in the debate. Stone argues through cogent visual images that Kennedy was shot by the CIA and its accomplices, and that their complicity was covered up by the Warren Commission.

The document needed for this exercise is the American University symposium "JFK: Cinema as History" (ID# 23934). Students can be provided with the transcript of the symposium to facilitate comprehension. Ideally, they will view *JFK* and read supplemental materials about the assassination and the Commission. The symposium brought together several prominent proponents of assassination theories. Admiral Fletcher Prouty argues that the CIA and military establishment had Kennedy killed. Author Dan Moldea argues that organized crime planned the hit. Representative Henry Gonzales, a member of the Commission, supports the Warren Commission and House Assassination Committee reports as the most credible alternatives.

Assign students to analyze the narrative accounts advanced by each speaker. This may be implemented in a variety of ways, ranging from individual or group research papers to the assignment of one student to each question for one narrator. Comparisons are facilitated by assigning each student one question to answer for each narrator. It is generally least advisable to assign one student to each narrator, since these speakers are convincing and the students generally uninformed. The following analytical framework, adapted from Fisher, is suggestive of the possibilities:

I. Narrative coherence:
   A. Argumentative or structural coherence:
      1. What central claims does the narrator want his audience to accept?

2. What evidence does he provide in support of each claim?
3. How does the narrator demonstrate that the evidence proves the claim? Is that warrant or connection explicitly stated by the narrator, or must the listener provide it?
B. Material coherence:
1. Which seemingly important facts does this account omit?
2. Which counterarguments does this account ignore or address?
3. Which seemingly relevant issues does this account overlook?
C. Characterological coherence:
1. Who are the central characters in this narrative?
2. Are they alleged to have behaved characteristically or unexpectedly?
3. What values or needs motivated characteristic behavior (and any deviation from it)?
II. Narrative fidelity:
A. What are the values stated or implied by the narrative?
B. Are those values appropriate to the decision the listener is being asked to make?
C. What would be the effects or consequences of living by these values?
1. for your self-concept?
2. for your own behavioral choices?
3. for your relationships with others and society?
4. for the rhetorical process?
D. Are these values affirmed in your personal experience?
1. In the lives of those you admire and respect?
2. In the judgment of your ideal audience for a persuasive speech?
E. Do the values constitute the ideal basis for human conduct?

The speakers address a variety of needs and issues. Admiral Prouty cynical and conspiratorial, urges Americans to "wake up" to the harsh realities of intelligence agencies and military power. He supports his case primarily with personal anecdotes that serve to enhance the credibility they might better undermine. Moldea documents his case against organized crime more carefully and challenges Prouty's handling of certain elements of the conspiracy. Representative Gonzales is the voice of reason, conceding that the Warren Commission's conclusions at times strain credulity, but insisting that they are less fantastic than the alternative explanations.

The Prouty and Moldea narratives dramatize fantasies about wealth and power, spies and racketeers, secret armies and hitmen—fantasies which have permeated novels, movies, and television for years. Gonzales's narrative emphasizes careful reasoning and is quite undramatic. A recurrent theme in the symposium is the need to open the

Warren Commission's files, but it is difficult to believe that any of these discussants will ever examine those files and conclude that he has been mistaken. The class may want to discuss Americans' inability to accept an undramatic explanation for such a dramatic and traumatic crime.

Finally, the exercise provides a good opportunity for students to discover how shared modes of reasoning lead to the formation of logical communities. It is interesting to have the class develop a narrative account of a controversy of the day—political money, an international crisis, or economic unrest—that speaks to the style of reasoning used by one of the JFK narrators. From there it is a short step to considering American politics as an ongoing conflict among incongruent logical communities.

Summary

The interpretive communities' approach to political communication blends intrapersonal cognitive processing, interpersonal relationship development, group and organizational cultures, societal integration, and rhetorical adaptation. It sets forth an overarching conceptual framework within which instructor and students can better understand politics by understanding how communication processes influence political behavior as well as how political processes influence rhetorical behavior.

The model can be covered quickly or used to frame the whole course, it can frame the students' reading of academic research or the development of their communication skills, and it can frame the study of normative or historically significant communication. It also permits the selection and synthesis of course readings that would otherwise seem conceptually incompatible.

Instructors at dog obedience schools tell us that they do not teach dogs to be obedient, they teach owners how to teach obedience. These exercises are suggestive of the ways that the interpretive systems approach to political communication can be taught. As you become familiar with the model and with these exercises try them with other tapes. Years ago I taught in a department that declined to purchase a sophisticated video projection system because it would have revealed flaws in our tapes. The tapes, except for rare historical footage, should be secondary to the theoretical points. Students at the turn of the century should be forgiven if they cease to relate to Ronald Reagan, Jerry Brown, Bruce Babbitt, or John F. Kennedy. They need to learn not that Babbitt used platitudes but that political figures employ a variety of languages that deserve our critical attention. Each week the C-SPAN network provides hours and hours of new examples with which to illustrate and test this approach. As we do so we can build and share an interesting database that can enrich and refine the interpretive systems model.

References

Bormann, E. G. (1972). Fantasy and rhetorical vision: The rhetorical criticism of social reality. *Quarterly Journal of Speech, 58*, 396-407.

Bormann, E. G. (1985). *The force of fantasy: Restoring the American dream.* Carbondale: Southern Illinois University Press.

Bosmajian, H. (1983). *The language of oppression.* Lanham, MD: University Press of America.

Delia, J. G. (1982). The constructivist approach to communication. In Frank E. X. Dance (Ed.), *Human Communication Theory.* New York: Harper and Row.

Fisher, W. R. (1987). *Human communication as narration: Toward a philosophy of reason, value, and action.* Columbia: University of South Carolina Press.

Maslow, A. L. (1943). A theory of human motivation. *Psychological Review, 50*, 370-396.

Schutz, W. (1958). *FIRO: A Three-Dimensional Theory of Interpersonal Behavior.* New York: Rinehart.

Smith, C. A. (1992, forthcoming). Master syllabus: The interpretive systems approach to teaching political communication. *Communication Education.*

Smith, C. A. (1990). *Political communication.* San Diego: Harcourt Brace Jovanovich.

■ 4

Two Courses that Treat of Women and Political Communication

Jane Blankenship

Political communication texts, for the most part, have ignored the growing importance of women in politics. However, as more women run for public offices it becomes necessary to address the special concerns they face as politicians. This chapter discusses the role C-SPAN can play in teaching students about women in politics. By focusing specifically on the speeches of Texas Governor, Ann Richards; the role of women in the Persian Gulf War debate; and the silencing of women in the Anita Hill/Clarence Thomas Hearings; students are introduced to the ways women are represented in politics.

Although women represent over half of the population and an increasing number of those running for electoral offices and holding offices, surprising little scholarship focuses on even major women public officials (including, for example, Supreme Court Justice Sandra Day O'Connor and Geraldine Ferraro, Democratic Party nominee for the Vice Presidency of the United States). Some political communication texts are beginning to include women not only as occasional examples of this or that, but they are also beginning to include some of the special problems women running for and holding public office have. Still, most course material in this area still needs to come from packages of material prepared by the classroom teacher.

During 1991-1992, I have taught two courses dealing in varying degrees with women and political communication: a three-credit course, Political Communication, and a three-credit course, Gender and Political Communication. Below I will outline portions of the two courses where I regularly use materials and briefly indicate the variety of ways I use those materials.

Six explicit assumptions underlie all of what follows below:

1) We co-construct our "political realities" in significant ways through communication.
2) The system we call a "political campaign" may usefully be viewed as a set of reciprocal agendas. The "players;" e.g., candidates, public, media, other institutions, all have a sense of what they want to accomplish and some priority ordering of these things. In a sense, all (although not equally) have certain things to "give" to each other in return for certain things they want to "get" from each other.
3) All political campaigns serve a variety of both symbolic and instrumental communicative functions.
4) Within all campaigns there are, at the macro and micro level, recurring forms such as announcement speeches, debates, apologia, metaphors, antitheses, parallel structure, and the like.
5) "Incumbency style" and "challenger style" have some substantial differences for both men and women.
6) Gender has major implications that permeate throughout every aspect of the campaign (and governance) process from establishing "credibility," to fundraising, to dealing with a language constructed almost exclusively by males whether that language be metaphorical (politics as war/combat and sports) or more "literal" (requisites such as "tough enough" to hold office), to dealing daily with an intricate maze of "double binds" as a result of such cultural constructions (women must be "tough enough" but not so "tough" as to be "unfeminine").

Political Communication

The primary focus of our political communication course is on how "political reality" is constructed through communication. This course examines domestic U.S. politics. To that end, we examine communication during particular political events—during acts of governance and campaign acts. During our discussion of communication and governance we examine presidential inaugurals, State of the Union addresses and responses, press conferences, and speeches at moments of crisis and triumph; Congressional hearings and debates such as those on the Gulf War and flag burning amendment; and Supreme Court decisions such as those involving abortion rights and during particular campaigns—most typically electoral campaigns. During our discussion of communication and campaigns, we look at single events (such as an announcement of candidacy, a debate, a press conference). We also examine small "systems of events" within the larger system of a full campaign (such as the forums/debates, and the television commercials of a given candidate). And, we examine whole campaigns as systems and as an integral part of our whole system of governance noting that campaigns may be temporary, but governance is ongoing. Moreover, our larger system of governance enables our electoral system and, in turn, is enabled by it. Thus, we view the whole electoral process as operating within the larger system, governance.

By the end of the semester students should have a better idea of the communication variables involved in political governance and campaigns, and some beginning notions of how those variables interact with one another. Readings are primarily from a "Selected Readings" multilithed booklet especially prepared for this course consisting of newspaper articles and magazine and journal articles, especially prepared handouts, and the text Political Campaign Communication, 2nd ed. by Judith Trent and Robert Friedenberg (1991).

Of course, it is clearly possible and, indeed, desirable, to include an entire unit specifically focusing on women and political communication (as well as integrating women rhetors throughout the class) in a number of courses. Since Political Communication is an "overview course," I include the topic as part of contexting changes in the political process highlighted by the 1990 "offyear" campaigns: (1) an increased number of women campaigning for higher office; (2) what analysts have termed the "new Black politics"; (3) wedge issues, such as abortion, and their relationships to single issue voting; and (4) increased early use of negative campaigning.

The unit focusing specifically on women candidates has a two-fold purpose: (a) to examine women as they participate in the regularly recurring forms of political communication, and (b) to explore some of the unique problems women often have as they campaign for electoral office.

In addition to certain chapters in Trent and Friedenberg, students read a report prepared by the Greenberg-Lake Analysis Group (1991) in Washington, D.C., "Campaigning in a Different Voice;" the Blankenship & Williams (1991) paper, "'Women' as Metaphor in Three 1990 Gubernatorial Campaigns;" and a variety of newspaper articles focusing on the candidacies of women, for example, "For Women, Better Climate is Seen" (1990).

The Greenberg-Lake report helps us focus on several compelling features of communicative life for women running for electoral office. Through debriefings of candidates, campaign managers and the like, they outline problems encountered and strategies for meeting those problems. For example, they point to the negative (not "tough enough" for the job) and positive ("honest" and "caring") stereotypes frequently attached to women candidates. They also detail the "double binds" of which I spoke earlier; for example, when women are required to attack or reply to an attack by their opponents, they must be "forceful" but not "shrill" or "bitchy."

The Blankenship and Williams paper focuses on the male constructed, male dominated lexicon into which women enter. They illustrate how several women running for governorships has come to deal with matters on definition and, particularly, redefinition by focusing on their use of such notions as nurturing, agent of change, transformer of values and the like.

In Political Communication we let students see, for example, women candidates participating in some macro and micro recurring forms (various types of speeches, debates, press conferences; using metaphors, antitheses, oxymorons) that are used by candidates generally, ask them to see if there are any unique features of women's discourse (such as types of metaphors), and also stress seeing women-at-work pursuing strategies to establish credibility, etc. Below, we will note materials used related to one candidate, Ann Richards (D, Texas). Materials include:

- [For background] Richards' "Keynote Speech" at the 1988 Democratic National Convention (ID# 3477).
- Richards' speech to the Texas Democratic State Convention (ID# 4646).
- [For contexting] Clayton Williams' speech to the Texas GOP State Convention (ID #13027).
- a representative "stump speech".
- TV commercials by both Richards and Williams.
- Richards-Williams' 8 minute debate on Education (ID# 140749).
- [For contexting, after election as an act of governance] Richards' "State of the State Address" (ID# 16675).

A reading such as "Texas Governor proves adept in her first year" (1992) is also a useful update. Readings about the campaigns can include additional articles from the national press, Texas newspapers, biographies and autobiographies, and book chapters (see "How Ann Richards got to be Governor of Texas" in Ivins (1991)). Student paper topics have included "Fundraising and women candidates," "Negative campaigning in the Texas Gubernatorial Race," "The role of humor in the campaign of Ann Richards," and "Differences and similarities between the campaigns of Ann Richards (Texas) and Dianne Feinstein (California)."

Gender and Political Communication

A second course, Gender and Political Communication, focuses not only on women campaigning for political office (contexted at least from the Vice-Presidential campaign of Geraldine Ferraro and the earlier 1972 presidential bid of Shirley Chisholm), but also on women in governance positions, and women outside of political office per se who are political observers (the media) and political activists (lobbyists, those in social movements), and so on.

During the Spring 1992 semester, the course focused on women communicating in three broad public arenas: (1) women campaigning for political office in 1990 and 1992; (2) women in Congressional settings (floor debate, Hearings, etc.); and (3) women talking about and being talked about in relation to the Gulf War. Since we have earlier touched on campaigning, below I will simply note several of the foci in (2) and (3). Of the Congressional communicative settings, we selected two specific "moments"—a floor debate over the President's ordering of troops into the Persian Gulf and Clarence Thomas' Confirmation Hearings before the Senate Judiciary Committee. C-SPAN tapes of both the floor debate and of the Confirmation Hearings in their entireties are readily available.

The central research question raised as we viewed the debate over the Gulf War was: In what ways, if any, did Congresswomen speak differently than Congressmen? We took as baseline concepts lines of argument, types of supporting materials ("proofs"), types of persons cited, and images/metaphors used. Deborah Robson, some of whose research focuses on this topic, provided us with a list of twenty-eight Congresswomen who were then paired with twenty-eight Congressmen according to party affiliation, state represented, and number of terms in office. Where no available matches occurred at the state level, comparable districts in other states were used.

Not only did the Confirmation Hearings for Judge Clarence Thomas to the Supreme Court provide us with yet a second congressional setting, it also provided us with an opportunity to examine other aspects of communicative behavior.

Since I have mentioned a number of ways to approach examining the "talk" of women running for and functioning in electoral office, here I will illustrate another way to use C-SPAN materials—as "text" (verbal and visual) for examining both the talk(ing) and silenc(ing) of women. Although there are abundant possibilities in examining Anita Hill's testimony during the Judiciary Committee Hearings for Clarence Thomas, below I will merely outline some of the silenc(ing) of women during a panel of four women arguing against confirmation before the testimony of Anita Hill.

In October, 1991, a panel consisting of Sarah Weddington, winning lawyer in Roe v. Wade; Kate Michelman, President, National Abortion Rights Action League; Fay Wattleton, President, Planned Parenthood; and Madeliene Kunin, former governor of Vermont—all four able and articulate women used to the public arena— testified concerning Judge Thomas' silence on Roe v. Wade C-SPAN covered this panel in its entirety—both opening statements and the question and answer periods which followed. Since the C-SPAN tape of this panel provides us with so many instances of silencing "strategies" (conscious and/or unconscious), below I will note only several different kinds readily observed by students.

First, before the panel said a single word, the scene in which the women spoke was one of silence in at least two pervasive ways: 1) the presiding committee, the Judiciary Committee, contained no women (only two women sit in our 100 person Senate) asking any questions from a position of power and, 2) the nominee, himself, had refused to answer earlier questions about his position on Roe vs. Wade. Indeed, Judge Thomas had maintained that he had not even casually talked about it at any point in his career.

By viewing this tape, students are able to point out the following: in their formal presentations the four women explicitly note these two powerful silences on which they must "play out" their roles. For example, former governor Kunin, given the most deferential treatment by the Senators as one of their own (an elected government official), says bluntly:

> Once again, when it comes to our issues we find ourselves repeating the ancient cycle of helplessness that women have experienced throughout history. The sense of powerlessness is painful. It is apparent right here in this room, where women are not equally represented in the decision-making process of this country. We are put in the position of pleaders, asking you to ask our questions for us . . . .

Some members of the Judiciary Committee used another strategy for silencing: they simply chose not to ask any questions of the panel thereby devaluing their experiences and allowing them potentially only the bare minimum of five minutes in which to state their arguments; e.g., Senator Thurmond thanks the "ladies" for coming but has no questions. The neutral "the panel" might have sufficed. But the decredentialing of the women occurs throughout in a variety of ways.

Students were able to spot these examples:

1) Sen. Specter silences members of the panel other than Kunin by stating in his third from the last comment, "Now Governor Kunin, your testimony has been significantly different from the other three women here today in that you have specifically stated you would not ask Judge Thomas for a statement as to how he would decide a

specific case and I infer from that that you mean you would not ask him to decide if he would uphold or reject Roe versus Wade." Specter cuts her off during her next comment but she responds more fully in the comment after that, "I am not satisfied that he [Judge Thomas] has come anywhere near giving us an indication of what his values are, what his general criteria are, and that would give us some indication of which general direction he is moving."

2) In Sen. Specter's last comment he claims to be paraphrasing Gov. Kunin's response when he says, "Well he has stated what he would do with Roe versus Wade. And you agree that that's acceptable." This is not what Gov. Kunin said nor what she meant. At the end of this comment Sen. Specter cedes the floor to the Chair, permitting no response.

3) In the same comment section by Sen. Specter he poses a question, "The questioning has taken him [Thomas] on quite a number of steps and speaking for myself, I would be interested to know just how far, how many of these questions he has to answer to give you the sense of assurance that you are looking for." He does not permit a reply. In addition he is silencing earlier testimony which had answered this question. Indeed much of the panel's testimony has focused on just this point.

4) In Sen. Brown's statement he silences Weddington by placing her in a hierarchy of women lawyers rather than lawyers, thus denying her full consubstantiality. He does so with the following narrative. "Miss Weddington, I particularly appreciated your relating your personal experiences. I think there are a good many Americans who simply are not familiar with the struggles women have had to go through, and your sharing your personal experiences, I think, is most helpful. My mother had school professors tell her that she was not welcome in their class and women were not welcome in the legal profession. It's been some years ago. But she's never forgotten it. And I think it's helpful for Americans to understand what it was like." He did not permit any responses to his comments.

5) In Sen. Simpson's 5th comment he silences the other members of the panel with the following comments, "And Governor Kunin, you are a politician. I know what you do, I know of you, admire your perseverance. You are the politician on this panel, the only one. And boy, there's a lot of difference between advocacy groups and politicians, I can tell you that."

An examination of the C-SPAN tape will reveal a number of other "silencing" strategies.

One can move from that Hearing room to examine other settings and other acts of silencing in an electoral setting, not the least of which is one used obviously and blatantly by Clayton Williams in his campaign against Ann Richards when he complained that she came from a "women's world" and he just "didn't know" how to talk with her. And for contexting purposes, one can refer to the C-SPAN tape of the 1984 Vice-Presidential debate and decredentializing strategies such as George Bush's failure to "name" her "Congresswomen Ferraro" which he had formally agreed to before the debate and, also, when given a chance by the debaters' moderator to ask Ferraro a direct question used two "exclusionary" strategies—first by saying he had no question to ask her and, then, by saying that perhaps the audience might like to talk about something else like "the World Series." A non-credentialed, non-jock warranted no question nor any answer-time.

The point in examining a number of women in a variety of settings will help to illuminate the pattern of silencing women and the various strategies for doing so. The examination will also help illuminate the varieties of ways women have for overcoming such strategies, for example, in the Thomas Hearings panel we discussed, the women interrupted each other and, therefore, they, collectively, got more "said" than had only one answered the question she was asked.

During the portion of the Gender and Political Communication course, which focuses on Women and the Gulf War, C-SPAN materials include a variety of Journalist Round Tables focusing on the Gulf including "Women Journalists on the Gulf War" (ID# 17285), and coverage of briefings by various governmental and military personnel. We have already noted our use of the floor debate on the Hamilton-Gephardt Resolution and the Solarz-Michel resolutions focusing on Gulf action. We further focused on how women soldiers talked about the War and were talked about on C-SPAN call-in shows. A particular interest of focus was the two week period immediately after the War. Eleanora Patterson's work, "The Slight 'Magics' of Gender" particularly informed our study. Here, we focused on how people quoted in the print media talked and the gender implications in their narratives and metaphors.

As can readily be noted from the brief descriptions above, many different kinds of C-SPAN material can be included in units or full courses focusing on women (and gender, more broadly) and political communication. That material provides a variety of texts (speeches, interviews, round tables, hearings, debates, television commercials) and both a special sense of immediacy and vividness to those texts. In our courses, we have used those texts to examine lines of argument, types of arguments (proofs), recurring forms, strategies for talking and silencing, the use of narratives, and language (e.g., metaphors) to examine public discourse, perhaps an especially urgent task for the discourse of hitherto underrepresented participants in the political process.

References

Blankenship, J.B. and Williams, M. (1991). "Women" as metaphor in three gubernatorial campaigns." Presented at the annual meeting of the Speech Communication Association, Atlanta, Georgia.

Greenberg, S. and Lake, C. (1988). *Campaigning in a different voice*. Washington, DC: The Analysis Group.

Ivins, M. (1991). *Molly Ivins can't say that, can she?* New York: Random House.

Lake, C. (1991). *Challenging the credibility gap: Executive summary, 1991*. Washington, DC: The Analysis Group.

Patterson, E. (1992, May 2). The benign metaphoric legacy of operation desert storm: The slight "magics" of gender. Paper presented at the annual meeting of the Eastern Communication Association.

Suro, R. (1992, January 19). Texas governor proves adept in her first year. *New York Times*, p. 10.

Toner, R. (1990, April 22). For women, better climate is seen. *New York Times*, p. 30.

Trent, J.S and Friedenberg, R.V. (1991). *Political campaign communication, 2nd ed.*. New York: Praeger.

■ 5

Public Action and the Environment

Star A. Muir

Preparing students for the twenty-first century will involve both shaping a vision of the future and instilling basic skills necessary to realize that vision. Addressing the problems of an eroding public sphere and the lack of effective public commitment, this essay explores C-SPAN as a resource for developing critical skills for public participation. Educators can use C-SPAN programming to teach students to organize critical arguments, to involve students in the political process, and to foster the practice of public argument. These exercises are useful for courses on the environment, for courses with sections focusing on environmental issues, or for a wide range of courses interested in developing critical thought, and organizational and presentational skills.

The task of an educator in modern times is a difficult one, plagued with great urgencies and constrained by information overload, economic realities and public apathy. Preparing students for the twenty-first century will involve both shaping a vision of the future and instilling basic skills necessary to realize that vision. Special challenges now face teachers hoping to increase awareness and empower action on issues that are often far removed from the student's world. The problems of global warming, ozone depletion, deforestation, solid waste disposal, water quality, air pollution and resource scarcity, to name a few, are difficult to convey to students interested in completing term papers, maintaining a high GPA, and getting a good paying job.

Enhancing and maintaining student awareness about critical issues, and taking that awareness to deeper levels of understanding and participatory action, are among the key challenges facing educators concerned with survival into and through the next century. This essay addresses C-SPAN's value in furthering this awareness, and explores C-SPAN as a tool both for teaching basic skills of organization and critical thinking and for empowering students to actively participate in local and national democratic processes.

The focus here is on environmental education, but the exercises and approaches can be easily applied to other issues, including public argument, political empowerment, and the general development of written and oral communication skills appropriate for an interested and active citizenry. Created in the context of an entire class devoted to the Rhetoric of Ecology, these exercises can also be integrated into broader courses as particular units or sections devoted to the environment. Environmental education should not be limited to classes on the environment, but can and should be integrated into other classes on political science, communication, history, English, journalism, and the rest of the curriculum. These approaches have, in fact, been used in classes on Argumentation Theory, Rhetorical Criticism, Small Group Processes, Public Speaking, and Persuasion.

The chapter outlines some important aspects of environmental awareness and education, and then provides specific illustrations of how C-SPAN can be useful in teaching environmental issues. The emphasis is on identifying specific problems faced by educators in a complex society, and on exploring creative ways to overcome these problems.

Environmental Education

There are essentially three features of public involvement that deserve specific mention: the erosion of public argument, the limitations of public awareness, and the gap between knowledge, commitment, and action. Each of these characteristics points, in turn, toward the utility of C-SPAN programming for the classroom.

A central concern for educators preparing students for the decades to come is the complexity of life faced by citizens in an era of scientific and technological expertise. As a by-product of industrial and technological development, environmental devastation is frequently intertwined with issues of scientific specialization and technical assessments of environmental impacts and costs. Hardin (1985), in his work *Filters Against Folly*, writes that the "greatest folly is to accept expert statements uncritically" (p. 11). Uncritical acceptance, however, often characterizes current student interactions with industry, government, and ecologists on information about the environment. Goodnight's (1982) distinction between technical, personal and public spheres of argument highlights this acceptance, emphasizing the ascendance of technical argument over viable forms of public dialogue. Ecology, Goodnight argues, started as public space, but quickly became subsumed as a science with an elite structure and an inaccessible vocabulary. Likewise, in their analysis of the accident at Three Mile Island, Farrell and Goodnight (1981) observe that deliberative and rational public discourse is abandoned in the techniques of mass manipulation and the patterns of technical communication that characterize the crisis.

In her description of *Eloquence in an Electronic Age*, Jamieson (1988) decries the increasing media use of the "synoptic" phrase, the quick sound bite that substitutes for audience dialogue with larger issues. In her view, debate is closed off, with a concomitant loss of public rationality, at precisely the point where auditors lose access to larger messages. With a focus on such "private" aspects of public discourse as a candidate's image, the arguments over public policy are overshadowed by the personal sphere. Unable to assess the overall coherence of a politician's argument, the citizenry becomes accustomed to shortened and summarized tidbits of information, and eventually may perceive this as how the political process functions.

This erosion of the public sphere, whether through an emphasis on the personal elements of public interaction, or through the ascendance of technical discourse, is significant for environmental communication and for education in general. Empowering students involves resurrecting such public space, by teaching skills for critically assessing messages shaped by the media, and by instilling confidence in grappling with technical jargon.

A second and related issue involves patterns of public awareness about critical issues. Labeled the decade of environmentalism, the 1990s is characterized by two main features of popular environmental discourse: the intertwining of economic motivation and environmental appeals in green consumerism, and the detailing of specific, tangible actions available to the individual agent (*50 Simple Things You Can do to Save the Earth*, 1989). Even with these trends in consumption and private activity, public awareness is not as consistent in this decade as originally anticipated. Distracted by the Persian Gulf War, and by the recession, environmental contributions have dropped considerably from previous levels (Lancaster, 1991). In the 1992 primary campaigns, environmentalism was essentially a nonissue; no candidate regularly raised the issue, and statements made in the campaign were largely reactive rather than proactive. The administration of the United States government has also, to date, opposed international agreements for limits on fossil fuel emissions of CO_2 ("Bush rejects emissions pact," 1992). The public voice on this issue has not been loud or sustained enough to force government action. The green movement, some fear, is losing the battle to save the earth (Walljasper, 1992).

One concern is that green consumerism and the "Things To Do" literature actually hamper awareness and action on the environment by restricting the scope of activity and creating a false sense of full participation. Cooperstein (1980) writes that while such "Earth hygiene" might raise your sense of self-esteem, "thinking you're doing enough to restore environmental balance is an illusion" (p. 15). By stressing convenience and consumption, these modes of relating to the environment may substitute for substantive citizen dialogue and political action, fostering a withdrawal from public life into the "cocoon of the personal and the private" (p. 15). Purchasing energy-conserving lightbulbs, for example, may constrain citizen action to economic participation, and reduce the probability of engaging the energy issue, and President Bush's energy policy, in the political arena. There is little argument, however, that these trends do result in greater awareness about environmental issues, in however simplified a fashion. Education must somehow bridge the gap between individual awareness and action by focusing attention on the means by which awareness in the personal sphere can be translated into public dialogue and active participation.

A final issue confronted by educators is the lag between political awareness, commitment, and action. The greenhouse issue, and the U.S. position on international limits on CO^2, is a clear example of how awareness by a growing number of scientists and organizations is not quickly translated into political commitment and action. Stressing the incapacity of the political subsystem to cope with the time frame of the ecological problem, Luhmann (1989) notes that the requirement for consensus in the political process reduces the probability that action will be taken. Part of the larger problem, Stapp and Polunin (1991) speculate, involves a "conceptual lag," a slowness to commit to making sacrifices for environmental gains:

> Conceptual lag is a quiet but influential force in carrying on traditional ideas and delaying the incorporation of new thoughts into a common frame of reference. Ideas and values are molded by past experience, and actions follow accordingly. Compounding this lag is the perpetuation of these deeply imbedded values through inherent reinforcement by government, schools, and other social institutions. (p. 14)

The problem, then, is both personal, in the acceptance of a different frame of reference *with its implications,* and institutional, in the fragmentation of political will on the environment. Education must account for both of these conceptions of lag, in trying to enable policy to catch up with critical needs, and in striving for commitment to action in more than one sphere of activity.

While the educational system is by no means solely responsible for coping with the erosion of the public sphere, the variability of current environmental attitudes, and the lag between awareness and action, educators do have a significant role to play in constructing a vision of the future and in teaching the skills necessary to move forward on that vision. As a direct access channel to public information on environmental issues, and to examples of the process of policy-making, C-SPAN can help to lessen these problems in several ways.

C-SPAN as an Educational Resource

From the many possible uses for C-SPAN in teaching awareness about environmental issues, three specific uses are identifiable to train skills necessary for coping with ecological and political complexities. Again, these exercises can be applied to other issues and concerns, or can be used on environmental issues as a section of a more general class.

Organizing Critical Arguments

The first approach to using C-SPAN for environmental education is to draw on samples of communication about the environment to instill a critical faculty in the students. The critical ability, in this exercise, is combined with efforts to teach organization and the clear layout of ideas and arguments. This "organizational exercise," very generally termed, involves watching a short segment of a public speech or pronouncement, generating critical ideas about the speech, and then organizing these ideas into a structured outline. Thus, the students critically assess an example of environmental communication, and then organize their ideas into a lucid outline. This exercise, in particular, is one of the most useful tools for teaching students in different types of classes to critically evaluate public information and to organize their ideas into a coherent package.

On December 3, 1989, William K. Reilly, administrator of the Environmental Protection Agency (EPA), delivered the Marshall address on the environment, his "Environmental Vision for the 1990s" (ID# 10051). The speech is an interesting effort by Reilly to establish his credentials as an environmental visionary and delineate some of the limitations he operates under at the EPA. A bit long for a regular class length, the speech has a concluding segment about ten minutes in length that is articulate, emotional, and posits some fairly concrete options. After watching this segment, and receiving some background to the speech (ten months in office,

Bush appointee, history of environmental positions), the students discuss the speech and make critical points about Reilly's persuasive effort.

The class is encouraged to focus on elements of persuasion that we have previously discussed, including the use of narrative and metaphor, the warranted relationship between claims and data, the careful construction of ethos, elements of ambiguity, the underlying values apparent in the appeals, and so on. Students are queried as to Reilly's effectiveness, his ethics, and the criteria used in making those judgments. In this example, Reilly tells two stories—one about a man burying himself in a coffin to raise money (addressing the budget deficit issue), and one about traveling to Germany to watch the collapse of the Berlin Wall. He tries to transform the environment/economy conflict by ethically and pragmatically prioritizing ecological wellbeing as essential for economic prosperity. He uses the metaphor of the flammable river, and implies that the EPA has "put out a lot of fires." All of these observations are written on the blackboard (or on the overhead projector, if available). Rather than just describing what happens in the speech, the focus is on critically assessing how the speech works, and whether it is effective for his audience.

Once a significant list of critical observations is generated, discussion turns to another topic: how would you organize these arguments into a coherent paper or report? Based on a handout of organizational principles, the class moves into deciding major points, making sure subpoints support major points, defining a thesis for the outline, labeling arguments and titles to sustain that thesis, and determining the order of the points. The full outline for the paper is generated in front of the class, and several suggestions are then made about how that outline, with additional supporting materials, would be translated into a full paper.

The exercise thus serves two functions: it fosters a critical perspective on public communication, and it enhances an ability to flexibly manipulate information and ideas to present to others. Trying to overcome the erosion of the public sphere, students directly grapple with issues, and are forced to assess the adequacy of claims, to evaluate the rhetorical uses of story and metaphor, and to discern the ambiguities of political rhetoric. Focusing on this speech and integrating it with more recent assessments of the administration's environmental policies, students are encouraged to engage the political arena on a continual basis, and build confidence in their own ability to critique material from experts in the field. They additionally build a capacity for organizing ideas and for maintaining some conceptual flexibility in viewing the issues, both key skills for effective participation in public affairs.

Another version of this exercise is to type out twelve to fifteen critical arguments about the speech (based on theoretical elements from class), and then have the students organize these statements into an outline to hand in for corrections. After the outline is corrected for organizational errors, students can view the speech and discuss the adequacy of the critical statements. This exercise can be used early in the class to correct problems with organizing ideas, and to familiarize students with what a critical argument looks like. The step beyond describing an environmental message or artifact, to critically assessing it based on some criteria or good reasons, is a difficult one for many students. Likewise, once students generate some critical ideas, they often have difficulty conceptualizing a way to communicate them clearly. By providing an example of critical assessment, which the students must grapple with in some depth as they organize it, these skills can be developed in conjunction.

Both of these approaches—the written assignment and the oral class exercise—can be used together, since giving students the set of arguments initially familiarizes them with critical statements, while organizing the discussed arguments empowers their critical abilities and reinforces good organizational skills. The C-SPAN network covers a variety of environmental speeches, conferences and presentations. All of these offer possibilities for in-depth analysis of arguments and claims on the environment. Generating a critical reading of how these messages work, along with honing organizational skills to effectively communicate that critical perspective, is a worthwhile application of C-SPAN coverage to the classroom.

Involving Students in the Political Process

The Purdue Archives offers a unique feature for dedicated teachers—compilations of selected C-SPAN programming. One of these compilation tapes focuses on an extended environmental conflict in Congress. The process whereby a bill becomes a law is outlined in great detail using the example of the Clean Air Act of 1990. There are thirteen individual tapes on the process, moving from previous committee action, to the role of interest groups, to the Senate floor agreement, to the House floor debate, to the final floor passage and the Presidential signing. The compilation tape (ID# 21100) consists of short summaries (ranging from four to fifteen minutes) of each part of the process.[1]

Using this tape as a background for how legislation is treated in Congress, and applying this knowledge to another example of congressional

---

1 Available from the Purdue Archives, the thirteen tapes total 10:29 hours of coverage, and sell for about $390.00. The compilation tape is 1:43, and sells for $49.95. If the whole package is purchased, the compilation tape only costs $19.95.

decision-making on the environment, students can engage the intricacies of the political system. Dividing into groups, the students choose a case study of an environmental bill or law, either historical or contemporary, and view the compilation tape outside of class. Using the Clean Air Act as a benchmark for comparison, groups present on the strategies, compromises and results of other legislative attempts. Several questions can be used to shape student research and the presentation of material in class:

1) What value conflicts are most obvious in the process? What are some subsidiary value questions?
2) What strategies are used by the major players in the action? Who is most effective? Why?
3) How is language used to construct particular positions? Outline a brief vocabulary, or glossary, of the environmental issue. Does it present unique problems? How is it mobilized by the parties involved?
4) What arguments are soundly constructed? Which are weak? Outline data-warrant-claim for several of the major arguments. Is evidence stronger for one side? Why?
5) What decision criteria (presumption, uncertainty, irreparability, etc.) are used or explicitly outlined by each side? Are they adequate?

These projects can be on environmental legislation such as the Clean Water Act of 1977, the Toxic Substance Control Act of 1976, and the Superfund of 1980, or perhaps on failed efforts like the National Energy Security Act of 1991, or even on recurring battles like the reauthorization of the Endangered Species Act. The presentation to the class provides background information, answers many of the questions raised above, and uses the Clean Air Act tape as a common area of knowledge for comparisons of key parts of the process. The compilation tape thus orients them to the process originally, and then operates as a resource to communicate about other environmental struggles.

The students learn about hard realities in a legislative system, begin to broach and operate within the specialized vocabularies of environmental science and of the political process, and start to make connections between personal environmental issues and public policy. Familiarity with the process, and with committed environmental groups operating within the process, is one way to overcome a "conceptual lag" between awareness, commitment and action. Consciously learning the vocabulary is a necessary first step toward empowerment. The compilation tape is a useful tool for managing both general familiarity and specific knowledge, and for bridging the private and the public spheres.

Practicing Argument

An interesting part of C-SPAN's service to the community is the call-in show that airs regularly. The subject matter of the call-in show varies, as does the format of the guest presentation. On August 23, 1990, C-SPAN presented an unstructured debate on the global warming issue and then opened up the lines for questions from callers around the U.S. and abroad (ID# 13655). Affirming the need for action on greenhouse gas emissions, Jeremy Leggett, Director for Science at Greenpeace, U.K., was opposed by S. Fred Singer, of the Washington Institute for Values in Public Policy, who underscored the uncertainty of the greenhouse effect and the risks of drastic action. Each made an opening statement, sparred wiht the other for a few minutes, and then continued the debate through a series of questions from viewers of the program.

The segment is useful in the classroom in several ways. Most notably, it grounds an interesting discussion on the greenhouse problem. Many of the relevant issues, including the measurements of warming, the fallibilities of computer models, the potential risks and benefits of warming, and the time frame of the various scenarios, are all discussed with clarity and fervor. The debate is heated and therefore of great interest to the students. Having already read material on the greenhouse effect, students are more willing to talk, and find themselves drawn into the debate by the intensity of the dispute.

A second effect of using this call-in segment is the connection made between abstract issues and individual concern and commitment. Hearing other citizens expressing opinions and engaging in dialogue on the environment, many with passion and knowledge, is stimulating for the students. Environmentalism as a citizen interest becomes less of an "out-there" and more of an "in-here," an "in-here" that is inextricably involved with issues that otherwise remain a far away "out-there." In his discussion on teaching *Environmental Advocacy*, Bryant (1990) urges a perceptual shift for students from being the object of knowledge to being a source of knowledge (p. 98). This call-in/debate format, unfamiliar to most students in its intensity and focus, is another way to build confidence in a student's capacity for effective participation.

Finally, as a sample debate on an environmental issue, the call-in segment can illustrate a model format for other in-class debates on environmental problems. The Timber Owl controversy, the renewal of the Endangered Species Act, cloth versus disposable diapers, styrofoam packaging versus paper, all of these issues are susceptible to debates between opposing value systems and differing interpretations of scientific research. All students are assigned to read material on the controversy, and then six are selected for each debate—two debaters and four panelists for initial questions. After three minute opening statements, panelist questions are addressed to the debaters for twenty minutes, and then the audience is invited to participate. These sessions typically run forty-five minutes, and can be assigned as a group option or on a voluntary extra-credit basis. The segment thus informs on the greenhouse issue and serves as a model for in-class interaction.

Conclusion

The organizational exercise, the group projects on the legislative process, and the mini-debates all involve skills that are essential for the development of an effective citizenry, skills that can be taught in any class on just about any subject. These skills are necessary in all fields of endeavor, but they are especially useful for enhancing awareness of ecological problems and encouraging participation in environmental policy. C-SPAN offers a unique resource to the teacher: broader and less distorted access to events in the political process, and coverage of many different forums and issues in the political arena. Used appropriately, this coverage can begin to overcome some of the difficulties outlined for achieving an aware and empowered citizenry. The public sphere can be reconstituted, but only with serious effort at reinvolvement, and at familiarization with key processes and terminologies. The transformation can be made between green consumption and green political participation, but close attention needs to be paid to personalizing the abstract and increasing. confidence in participatory skills. The gap between awareness, commitment and action can be bridged, but nothing less than a sustained effort on the part of the educational system has a chance of long-term success.

A challenge needs to be issued, of course, for C-SPAN to increase its coverage of environmental issues, including reporting U.S. statements made in international conferences, and paying closer attention to alternative viewpoints on environmental policies. More is better, and there does need to be more. The responsibility for effective use of C-SPAN, however, lies with educators across the nation and around the world. The twenty-first century is coming fast.

References

Bryant, B. (1990). *Environmental advocacy: Concepts, issues, and dilemmas.* Ann Arbor, MI: Caddo Gap Press.

Bush rejects emissions pact, may skip "Earth summit" (1992, March 28). *Washington Post,* p. A8.

Clean Air Act highlight compilation (1991). ID# 21100.

Cooperstein, B. (1990, April 22). Earth day: Color it green. *Los Angeles Times Book Review*, p. 15.

Global warming changes (1992). C-SPAN call-in show. ID# 13655.

Earth Works (1989). *50 simple things you can do to save the Earth*. Berkeley, CA: Earthworks Group.

Farrell, T. & Goodnight, G.T. (1981). Accidental rhetoric: The root metaphors of Three Mile Island. *Communication Monographs, 48*, 271-300.

Goodnight, G.T. (1982). The personal, technical, and public spheres of argument: A speculative inquiry into the art of public deliberation. *Journal of the American Forensic Association, 18*, 214-227.

Hardin, G. (1985). *Filters against folly: How to survive despite economists, ecologists, and the merely eloquent*. New York: Penguin Books.

Jamieson, K. H. (1988). *Eloquence in an electronic age*. New York: Oxford University Press.

Lancaster, J. (1991, February 15). War and recession taking toll on national environmental organizations. *Washington Post*, p. A3.

Luhmann, N. (1989). *Ecological communication* (John Bednarz, Jr., Trans.). Chicago: University of Chicago Press.

Reilly, W. K. (1989). *An environmental vision for the 1990s* (ID# 10051).

Stapp, W., & Polunin, N. (1991). Global environmental education: Towards a way of thinking and acting. *Environmental Conservation, 18*, 13-18.

Walljasper, J. (1992, March/April). The anti-green backlash. *Utne Reader, 50*, 158-159.

☐ Part II
Developing Skills

■ 6
Teaching the Business and Professional Speaking Class

Lawrence W. Hugenberg

C-SPAN broadcasts can be helpful teaching aids in the business and professional speaking course. Videotapes can be edited into useful bites of video to illustrate small, but important, elements of presentational speaking preparation and delivery. Broadcasts can also be used in their entirety to demonstrate how all the small elements explained in textbooks and class discussion come together as a complete presentation. This essay explains how to use videotape segments or complete speeches to help students better understand specific elements of presentational speaking and group presentations. The essay discusses the preparation of videotapes for classroom use and explains the benefits for students who witness use of specific techniques and strategies in actual presentations.

One difficult task for the instructor teaching business and professional speaking is illustrating to students the types of communication situations they are likely to encounter in their careers. Locating examples of professional communicators facing real audiences in real business situations is challenging. Too often speech teachers attempt to illustrate how presentations are delivered in business settings by using student speeches taped in previous classes. Sometimes instructors will ask an area professional to come to class to deliver a presentation. Although these teaching strategies may be helpful, they do not substitute for examples of actual presentations delivered to business audiences. Accumulating tapes of actual presentations to use in the business and professional speaking class can be facilitated with access to C-SPAN broadcasts.

Uses in the Business and Professional Speaking Course

There are multiple uses for C-SPAN materials in the business and professional speaking course. In my class, I use excerpts of presentations (e.g., "Special Order" sessions in the House of Representatives, speeches to the National Press Club, news briefings by Cabinet members and/or their spokespersons, news conferences, etc.) to illustrate specific points throughout the term, and videotapes of entire professional presentations late in the term. After collecting hours of videotaped presentations from C-SPAN broadcasts, I identify parts of those presentations that illustrate specific points related to presentational speaking. Once identified, the similar components (e.g., introductions, uses of humor, transitions, conclusions, uses of statistics, emotional appeals, personal testimony, etc.) are edited on to separate tapes. Each tape illustrates a particular element of preparing and delivering a presentation.

Preparing Videotape Segments

The taped presentations are edited into short segments for use during the term. Usually no longer than three minutes, each includes multiple examples of important elements of presentational speaking so students see different speakers using these strategies during presentations. To prepare these tapes, I use advanced telecommunications students to help edit them into useful formats for the business and professional speaking class.

Thus far, I have developed tapes that illustrate the following elements of presentational speaking:

1) Using Supporting Materials (e.g., statistics, quotations, examples, etc.)
2) Using Visual Aids
3) Using Transition Materials
4) Using Oral Footnotes
5) Developing Conclusions
6) Using Figures of Speech
7) Developing Introductions
8) Creating Appropriate Language Strategies

Students should prepare for the class sessions when the tapes are to be used. They should read appropriate chapters in the textbook, and instructors should lead class discussions on relevant elements of presentational speaking. For example, when the class is discussing how to begin a presentation, I play a videotape with different types of introductions from actual presentations to illustrate important points, such as gaining the audience's attention, previewing the presentation, stating the thesis statement, establishing personal credibility and giving a transition to the body of the presentation. To illustrate the use of emotive language, I have shown excerpts from Louis Farrakhan's speech, "Blacks in Government" (ID# 8766) and some of the passionate speeches made by members of the House of Representatives and the Senate during the debates to authorize the use of U.S. military in the Persian Gulf against Iraq. A good class discussion usually follows each example from the videotape regarding how "good" or "bad" the specific video segment was. In addition, these discussions help the instructor test her or his reasons for selecting a particular set of examples for classroom use.

The results of using examples of specific aspects of presentational speaking are extremely encouraging. The quality of students' presentations has improved dramatically in my business and professional speaking classes. These improvements are especially noticeable in the students' use of documented evidence to support assertions *and* in the quality of their visual aids used during a presentation. A good source for illustrating these principles has been the news briefings by the Defense Department spokespersons and military personnel during the Gulf War. It is one thing to explain proper ways to do specific speaking techniques or strategies to students when preparing them for their speaking assignments. It is entirely different (and, I think, better) to show them that actual communicators effectively use these strategies and techniques in their presentations to business audiences.

Using Entire Presentations

Another class exercise using presentations from C-SPAN is to play an entire presentation and discuss it during class. For this exercise, it is important that the tape take no longer than half the class period, leaving enough time for class discussion. This is important so the discussion of the presentation occurs while it is fresh in the students' minds. Speeches delivered by members of Congress during the "Special Orders" sessions are useful because the time limits imposed by the rules of the House of Representatives limit the length of the members' speeches. These sessions can be videotaped almost anytime the House is not in regular session.

The discussions that follow the videotape focus on what the speaker did that was "good" and what the speaker did that was "not so good." Inevitably students disagree on their evaluations of the presentation, thus providing the instructor an opportunity to highlight the importance of audience analysis and the fact that, no matter what students do as speakers, they will not please everyone in the audience. These videotapes help illustrate how each part of the presentation fits together or fails to fit together into a complete and refined presentation. Any tape can be stopped to highlight particular points, to make comments about what the speaker did in the presentation, and/or begin a discussion about the students' presentation assignments.

These class discussion sessions are valuable in two additional ways. First, if the instructor has a tape of a persuasive presentation and an informative presentation, he or she can use them to help clarify assignment directions prior to the students working on their persuasive and informative presentations. The instructor, in previewing the tapes before using them in class, can prepare appropriate comments and questions to make the assignment specifications clear to the students. These sessions contribute to the noted improvement of the presentations in my classes because students have seen how the directions for each assignment operate in an actual presentation.

Second, one of the most helpful sessions for students/speakers in communication performance courses is to critique other students' presentations. The C-SPAN tapes are used to train students to be better listeners to the content **and** delivery aspects of a presentation. There are many different types of critique sheets available to use when listening to presentations. If provided critique sheets prior to watching a student presentation, each student can serve as critic during the in-class presentation, and the instructor can lead a discussion on what the students highlighted in their critiques.

The Panel Discussion

Many C-SPAN broadcasts are panel discussions (e.g., National Science Foundation presentations, the National Endowment of the Arts, Congressional hearings, the deliberations of the Small Business Administration, etc.) of group presentations by members of government agencies, congressional committees and business forums. The panel discussion and group presentation is a difficult assignment to teach students in the business and professional speaking course. By taping several panel discussions and group presentations from C-SPAN, instructors have multiple examples of skills to highlight in lectures, and illustrations for students to learn from when preparing for their panel discussions and group presentations. The instructor can then follow the same instructional practices outlined for presentational speaking already discussed in this essay.

Working in groups to prepare a discussion has proven to be the most difficult assignment in my business and professional speaking classes. Students frequently moan: "I'm doing all the work and my grade depends on how well other students do"; "I don't have time to work in a group; can't I do another individual presentation?"; or "There isn't enough information for an entire group presentation." It takes a strong commitment by the instructor to make the group assignment a successful learning experience. Videotaped panel discussions and group presentations from C-SPAN assist both student and instructor in developing this assignment

By using a lengthy segment of a panel discussion or group presentation (20-25 minutes), students witness the flow of the actual discussion or presentation. They witness the qualities of turn-taking, supplying information, seeking clarification, making statements, asking questions, dealing with conflict, offering transitions between presentations, stating internal summaries of particular points of view, and reaching resolution. These videotape segments supplement instructors' lecturing on the fundamentals of preparing for and participating in group discussions. They make the lecture material clearer—easier to understand than hours of additional class lecture and discussion.

Conclusion

To help students understand individual elements of presentations and how they work together to form a complete presentation, C-SPAN offers the instructor tremendous latitude in highlighting specific elements of presentational speaking. Isolating these elements is extremely helpful when illustrating to students how people use different communication strategies in developing, supporting, and delivering presentations. After reviewing and discussing the individual elements and strategies, the instructor can show how the elements fit together in to a presentation by using complete business presentations and groups broadcast by C-SPAN.

The applications of the material broadcast by C-SPAN are unlimited in the business and professional speaking course. For example, if the instructor wants to work on interviewing techniques, C-SPAN broadcasts interviews which can be dissected into specific questioning and response strategies just like the presentations are dissected into component parts. C-SPAN broadcasts can be used in class to illustrate "good" and "not so good" communication situations that fit any assignment in the business and professional speaking course.

The rewards of using C-SPAN tapes for students and instructors of the business and professional speaking course are well worth the effort of reviewing and editing the tapes for classroom use. Students gain insight into how professional presentations are delivered. As a result, the quality of their presentations in the business and professional speaking class has improved. Instructors are able to highlight specific speaking tips before a round of presentations begin. After the round is over, the instructor can review points identified as particularly weak or missing during the students' presentations. Students and instructors enjoy the opportunity to witness textbook and lecture material come to life in these videotapes.

■ 7

Teaching Parliamentary Procedure

Don M. Boileau

This essay identifies several uses for C-SPAN programming in teaching students how to effectively operate under parliamentary rules. Programs such as the coverage of the British Parliament question and answer time are identified with specific applications for the classroom. Particular techniques are then discussed to maximize the use of the programming in fostering student understanding and appreciation of formal and informal elements in parliamentary proceedings.

The order of business is announced by the man with the powdered wig while a roar of attention seeking-requests begins. Prime Minister John Major stands on his party's side of the House of Commons to answer questions posed by members of the British Parliament. This process can be seen weekly on C-SPAN's program, "Question Time in the British Parliament." Although a prescribed order exists for this question period, most of the students watching for the first time will note that the process seems to be chaotic. What they are viewing on videotape is a far cry from the early mimicking of meetings they have experienced in a beginning one-hour "Introduction to Parliamentary Procedure Class." While this perceived chaotic tension in parliament is one of my primary objectives in showing this segment, C-SPAN provides a visual example which can teach the application of parliamentary motions (amend, send to committee, adjourn), procedures (precedence, one motion at a time, speaking order), and principles (majority rule, minority rights).

Since parliamentary procedure is taught in a variety of configurations (workshops and one-to-three hour courses) this explanation will outline ways an instructor might use C-SPAN for both enrichment and direct teaching purposes. The class at George Mason University is a one-semester hour course with emphasis on learning how to use parliamentary procedure in chairing meetings. Thus, watching the House of Commons questioning period allows the students to see a leader facing a difficult situation in which the parliamentary rules are vigorously followed. Since teachers can adapt any curricular example to a variety of teaching objectives, specific applications of some C-SPAN programs will be discussed as either models for replication or a starting point for the reader's creative applications.

Programs and Applications

Question Time in the British Parliament

Parliamentary procedure in its very name suggests the historical roots of the traditions that form the background for the philosophical traditions of the class. Thus, the opportunity to visualize the system that spawned America's use of *Roberts Rules of Procedure* is justification alone to show some segments of the British parliament in action. In fact, this was the original intent of the author in showing a segment of the show.

The robes, wig, and position of the speaker suggest a tradition that spans centuries. The fact that the Prime Minister is seated among the members emphasizes that she or he is an elected member of parliament—a contrast to our system with its division of powers among the executive, judicial, and legislative branches. For most meetings students will participate in, the presiding officer will be a member of the body, hence just the appearance of the Prime Minister to answer questions allows a discussion of the voting rights and obligations of the presiding officer.

The British questioning period provides a visual image of the physical layout of parliament—in itself a wonderful stimulus for a discussion of using space in meetings as well as the way space contributes to the order of inquiries. Viewing parliament's physical layout, one can easily see how it emphasizes turn taking, especially the principle of alternating speakers on the sides of an issue. Students immediately see how easy it is in the British House of Commons to identify what side of an issue a speaker might be by the seating arrangement—a major contrast to the average P.T.A., community association meeting, or even our class meetings. I also use this opportunity to explain how in large meetings where representation is by state, and not political ideology (House of Commons, U.S. Senate), organizations often use color coded cards to identify positions on issues, i.e., the National Education Association. For many students, seeing the British House of Commons in action is by far the most visual example of the impact of space on this principle, especially because of the quality camera work.

While the questioning period is not one for enacting legislation, it does provide examples of several aspects of running and participating in a meeting. The first surprise for most students is the noise of parliament in both the attempts to be recognized and the responses of members to speeches and questions. This major contrast with our legislative bodies is instructive as it raises the importance of decorum and the role of the presiding officer. For many of my students the subtle message is that they can be far more assertive without being disruptive, since the rules emphasize that only one person at a time has the floor. The importance of one person having the floor becomes clear as they watch questioner after questioner finish the inquiry. The role of "back benchers" (a new member of parliament who by custom sits in the very last row) as well as the use of the term provides additional discussion on the relationship of space and order of speaking. I use it to mention the role of the "maiden speech" and, particularly, the great shame that Winston Churchill felt in blanking out in the middle of his initial speech to the House of Commons.

Students quickly pick up the way the Prime Minister uses notebooks with information to help answer questions. The quick pace of questions and answers also helps the discussion of time limits during any session. The speed with which the questions are asked and answered not only speaks to the issue of preparation, but it also demonstrates how following the rules allows a tremendous amount of information to be presented.

Because any class is not limited to only the issues of the parliamentary procedure, other key concerns are visually apparent for students to notice, especially the current topic of the scarcity of female members in parliament and/or Congress. This message is common in most legislative bodies. In the George Mason location, I remind students to look at our school board meetings, which are also on cable. Since the local school district is one of the ten largest school districts in the United States, observers can see a powerful legislative group dominated by female members (only four males of the eleven members).

Because one finds in the questioning period a considerable amount of evidence in both the questions and answers, the efficient use of time for argument becomes a question worth pursuing for the parliamentary procedure class. While my course does not concentrate on the development of speeches, because of the limited time in a one hour class, this program does provide instructional models in parliamentary speaking. As parliamentarian for the Association of Teacher Educators, I developed a guide for beginning speakers urging them to identify their position (for, opposed, not sure) in their opening ("I support this resolution..."), or identify the parliamentary action being proposed for the body to consider ("I move to amend...", "Point of Personal Privilege...", "I move to send this motion to a committee...", etc.), and then immediately provide the evidence that supports their position. This C-SPAN program helps introduce this issue.

Prime Minister Major in answering questions often assumes the burden of proof, so he quickly marshals opinion, facts, and positions of his government into his answers. Although this class is not one in argumentation, this program provides a most helpful beginning model of what can be done to support assertions. My class includes a variety of topics on which no advance notice is given, so students quickly learn to search their experience to support their positions.

Equally valuable is learning how to use parliamentary procedure to prevent action from being taken without adequate information. Thus, this observation from the British parliament provides a reminder of the motions postponing action to a definite time, referring to a committee, tabling, and postponing indefinitely.

Congressional Hearings

Although these presentations (listed in the Public Affairs Video Archives guide under "Senate Committee" or "House Committee") consist mainly of a) lengthy statements, and b) question/answer sequences, hearings provide useful examples of several principles of parliamentary procedure. First, the concept of one person having the floor at a time is utilized. One can use the actions of the chair as the presiding officer to note how control of the floor moves among the chair, the witness, and the committee members.

Hearings also allow one to emphasize the clarifying role of questions, as panel members are often asking questions about the meaning of information presented. These models are helpful examples of what one can do with points of information in regular meetings—the principle of clarification is being illustrated in a different setting. Just as the members often get into long, complicated questions that are almost impossible for a witness to answer, a student in class can fall into the same trap. Thus, during a hearing examples of a precise, concise question provide good models for a parliamentary procedure class.

U.S. House and Senate Sessions

While the rules of both the House and Senate differ from Roberts—an observation itself that is valuable—the principles remain the same: majority rule, minority rights, one issue at a time, a precedence of motions, rules of decorum and procedure, and respect for others. The exact application by the instructor will vary with the session. These sessions (listed in the Public Affairs Video Archives guide as "House Proceedings" or "Senate Proceedings") provide an interesting contrast from class sessions based on Roberts (or other parliamentary manuals such as those authored by Sturgis or Riddick).

The respect embedded in the language of formal address by members of both houses of our legislature provides a good model for students. The discussion of respect by forms of address and reference to other members was not as important an issue five years ago as it seems to be today. Models of disrespect are more likely to be in the news, while models of respectful discourse are often edited out because of limited newscast time. The use of C-SPAN programs from the House and Senate provides good models for students regarding the respectful forms of address to the chair and to each other. By using debates on highly emotional issues, such as flag-burning, the confirmation of Justice Thomas, and the Gulf War Resolution, the classroom teacher can point out these forms of address in contrast to later arguments made by the speakers.

Congressional sessions sometimes are good models of the amending process, particularly as a significant bill comes to the floor. Besides the primary and secondary restrictions of Roberts, the congressional rules of debate influence amendments. By observing these debates, students can learn how a planned sequence of amendments might be used to enhance or kill a bill. Political strategy needs to be addressed in parliamentary procedure in a way that parliamentary procedure textbooks often avoid. A particular procedure in a congressional debate featured on C-SPAN can illustrate the important blend of politics and procedure.

Classroom Procedures

In planning the use of C-SPAN tapes, the principles of audio-visual application still apply: a) indicate at the beginning of the session what to look for, b) review the tape before it is shown to help in answering questions, c) include a debriefing session at the end to highlight certain aspects of the viewing, and d) plan an alternative action in case of machine failure.

On an overhead (or the blackboard) list the key ideas for students to observe. For example, the following seven items can be used to set up class observation and discussion:

1) The symbols of power of the Speaker
2) The physical arrangement of the House of Commons
3) The order of questions
4) How aides help provide the Prime Minister information to answer questions

5) The noise level: getting recognition and responding to comments
6) Participation by back benchers
7) The role of women

This outline reinforces remarks and structures the debriefing sessions. One can also write comments on the overhead (or blackboard) during the presentation if a particular issue relating to a previous classroom experience develops. For example, in February of 1992 the economy in Britain was the focus of one session. Competing examples of the success or stress in the economy were embedded in the questions and the Prime Minister's responses. Students could note the way Major answered the specific example of interest rates with the general performance of the economy. This action allowed a classroom discussion of politics and parliamentary strategy from an earlier session to be recalled by the instructor.

Another way to use these tapes is to have a student go to the board and record what the students observe as the principles and motions being used in the video presentations. Two students can be used, one for motions and one for principles, to set up the review. The instructor can add other items after the students' list is completed and discussed. This approach is particularly helpful when a large number and variety of motions are presented.

Summary

C-SPAN's visual examples stimulate many topics for a parliamentary procedure class. In just the areas of space and visual appearances alone, topics can be enhanced by C-SPAN use that take far time to try to explain by lecture. The C-SPAN programs allow topics to be quickly covered, while other aspects of the tapes can introduce new concepts.

The other great advantage of tapes is that one can stop the tape to make specific remarks. One function of stopping the tape is to raise the question as to how one would achieve the same function in our own class meetings. The specific adaptation is immediately demonstrated rather than waiting for a later time, or hoping that the students perceive the same adaptation that the instructor does.

C-SPAN offers a unique vantage point for students of parliamentary procedure: access to arguments, emotions, and heated exchanges of decision-makers engaged in fierce conflict under strict procedural rules. Gaining an understanding of how the rules operate is useful for students, but gaining an appreciation of the value and function of the process in real life is invaluable.

References

Riddick, F.M. (1991). *Riddick's rules of procedures*. Lanham, MD: University Press of America.

Roberts, H.M. (1989). *Roberts' rules of order*. New York: Berkeley Books.

Sturgis, A. (1966). *Sturgis standard code of parliamentary procedure, 2nd ed*. New York: McGraw-Hill.

■ 8

Teaching Persuasion

David R. Neumann

This essay discusses five exercises using C-SPAN to focus on persuasion. Each exercise focuses on a specific topic central to persuasion in an electronically-mediated society: language choice, nonverbal communication, demographics, attitude change, and media agenda setting. The goal of each exercise is to bring new and exciting material into the classroom, to stimulate student interest and discussion, and to expose students to the impact of persuasion on public policy making.

Teaching courses in persuasion affords the instructor a great deal of latitude in subject matter. Persuasion can be examined from intrapersonal and interpersonal to political and international contexts, and within these contexts many areas can be covered. In most persuasion courses and text books the following areas are discussed: language choice, nonverbal communication, demographics, attitude change, and media agenda setting.

The following descriptions are skeletal structures of exercises that can fit many educational formats, from small highly interactive seminars up to large lecture hall classes. The course I teach seats twenty-five to thirty-five students per section. Exercises and class discussions are run with the class as a whole or broken down into small groups of five to seven students. The focus of the course is on persuasion from a receiver's perspective: the main goal is for students to raise their personal awareness of how significant persuasive messages are in society and how to understand the many elements of persuasion when making decisions. The following exercises isolate several elements inherent to most mass persuasion. Using C-SPAN and other public affairs publications adds balance to this course which emphasizes advertising and corporate persuasion.

Various Exercises

Language Choice

This exercise focuses on the language choice of public policy makers and influencers. Show your class a selection of highly charged discourses such as *"At the Feeding Frenzy"* forum (ID# 5539) which focuses on biased press coverage and its affects on peoples' careers. President Bush's "Liberation of Kuwait" address (ID# 15723) or any National Press Club speech can also be used for more timely examples. Instruct students to list emotionally charged and value-laden terms used by the speaker. Then have the students rewrite the messages using synonymous terms that have a more neutral tone. Next show a selection of messages that are delivered in a more neutral tone and have the student rewrite the message with more emotionally charged language. Have a student or two volunteer to deliver these altered addresses to the class. This exercise helps students to identify and experience the power of language.

Nonverbal Communication

Arguably more important than the actual language of persuasive messages, are the nonverbal elements of the communication. This exercise orients the students to their own biases when it comes to judging a speaker's persuasiveness based on nonverbal image. Nonverbal communication includes all elements of the message beyond words including gestures and eye contact to clothing and hair styles. An excellent tape to use is the "Texas v. Johnson Arguments" (ID# 6846) where various "anti-establishment looking people" challenge the bill to make flag burning a felony offense. Show a videotape of a speaker with the audio turned down. Ask students to respond to various questions concerning their perceptions of the speaker based on visual cues alone. These questions could include the following: How convicted was the speaker to the issue or message? How convincing was the speaker? Does the speaker have a regional accent or dialect? How believable and credible was the speaker? Next, replay the same segment with the audio turned up to check students' accuracy in their prediction based on nonverbal cues alone. Then engage the class in a discussion of the impact of nonverbal communication on our perceptions of the entire message.

Demographic Profiles of Policy Makers and Influencers

Assign students various dates and times to view C-SPAN with the goal of creating demographic profiles of policy makers. Have them view regularly scheduled programs such as "America and the Courts," "Booknotes," "Communications Today," "Event of the Day," "National Press Club speeches," "Road to the White House," and "Short Subjects." Students should watch C-SPAN during their assigned times to make note of the sex, age, race, geographical background and other objective information of the policy makers and influencers. In a future class combine all of the students' data. Discuss how predictable the results were and what influence the results might have on policy decisions. Results from this exercise usually confirm the students' assumption that wealthy-looking, fifty- to seventy-year-old, somewhat attractive, white males account for most of the policy-making and influencing. Interesting discussions of the consequence of this perceived homogeneous group usually follow.

Attitude Change

Show a tape of a C-SPAN debate in class. Three excellent debates to use are the Parents' Music Resource Center's attempt to force record companies the add caution labels to some records, the debates concerning flag burning (ID# 17085 & 17086), and the "Dan Rather interview of George Bush" (ID# 752). After each speaker, or after each few minutes of discourse, have student's report on their attitudes about the topic. This should be done first through an object evaluation form that should be made up based on the examples chosen. A suitable evaluation form is a simple semantic differential scale with opposite terms at either end of a continuum: like/dislike; agree/disagree; honest/dishonest; trustworthy/not trustworthy; rational/irrational; intelligent/unintelligent. Next lead the class in either small group or entire class discussions concerning their responses. This feedback can be used to isolate issues, arguments, and delivery styles that seem to have the most persuasive effect. In the past students were quite surprised how their own attitudes were swayed, even on issues they well versed in.

Current Events Agenda Setting

Break the class up into five groups and assign one of the following networks to each group: C-SPAN, ABC, NBC, CBS, CNN. Have the individuals from each group tune exclusively into their assigned networks during national news broadcasts as homework. The C-SPAN group should view the "Event of the Day." In the following class allow the groups to discuss the major events of the day; have them rank the events by their level of importance. Next have them discuss the details of information gained about the events from the broadcast. In the past, the ensuing discussion has revealed that the C-SPAN viewers only had one issue to discuss, but were able to do so in detail. Class discussions then turned to who decides what is news, whether it is better to have more stories and less detail or visa versa, etc. By having the five groups compare their different rankings, students can develop a clearer picture of the impact of agenda setting on "objective" news sources.

Conclusion

These exercises can be helpful in clarifying course concepts and generating lively interaction. They also serve to increase students' awareness of current events and develop a greater sense of how public policy makers and influencers operate. For the purposes of teaching persuasion, these exercises allow for the isolation and detailed discussion of various aspects of persuasive communication.

References

At the feeding frenzy (1988, October 19). ID# 5539.

Dan Rather interview with George Bush (1988, January 25). ID# 752.

Flag amendment debate (1990, June 19). ID# 17085, 17086.

Presidential address (1991, January 16). ID# 15723.

Raised on rock and roll (1987, October 26). Parents' Music Resource Center. ID# 1184.

Texas v. Johnson arguments (1989, March 24). ID# 6846.

☐ Part III
Understanding Media

■ 9
C-SPAN, A Place for Student Analysis and Discovery

Kenneth E. Hadwiger and Amy C. Paul

Using C-SPAN programming as the context of certain classes is valuable, but in some classes dealing with mass communication, C-SPAN, itself, becomes a valuable topic of study. When viewed as a unique communication concept among similar technologies, C-SPAN's public service agenda is worthy of student attention. After their initial reluctance to be involved with useful television programming, students usually are receptive to the C-SPAN network.

Even at this relatively advanced stage of my life, I can remember sitting as an undergraduate in those large, General Education classes. Reams of locally printed handouts, mostly anonymous "mimeos" or "liths," were distributed up and down the aisles of the large auditoriums. After the Professor finished discussing them in class, we tucked them, sloppily, in our notebooks. Some never again saw the light of day. A few received a cursory review during final exam week. Then they were stored with the notebooks that held them, never to be seen again until about the 15th class reunion, when they were unearthed along with other memorabilia.

I suspect that much of the C-SPAN programming used in classrooms suffers a similar, nameless fate. You can't even stuff C-SPAN in your notebook! Too often, in my experience, students are impressed by the C-SPAN video I show them in class, but they don't have the foggiest idea where that footage came from a week later. But then, I don't remember where any of those mimeos or liths came from either.

The undergraduate students in my media classes often do not bring with them a good idea of what C-SPAN is or does. That always amazes me, probably because I am such a fan of the network. However, during a recent C-SPAN Seminar for Professors, I discovered that my classes were not unique in that respect. Most professors at the seminar seemed to spend more time and energy introducing students to C-SPAN programming than to the medium of C-SPAN.

We seem to assume that C-SPAN programming is a source of content primarily for instructors to bring to the classroom. Our litany of ways to use C-SPAN nearly overlooks the possibility that our students might learn directly from C-SPAN on their own, if they know more about what and where it is. Consequently, this essay is offered as a reminder that C-SPAN's contribution to our classrooms is more than just a source for "video handouts" from the Professor. It also can be a direct, primary source of information for media students to browse, perhaps for a lifetime.

A favorite assignment in my undergraduate classes on new mass communication technologies is a small group report on "What C-SPAN Is." Clustered with reports by other student groups in the class on WorldNet (the USIA's global satellite network), Illinet (our state-wide university library card catalog and topic/author search system), and InterNet (the world wide computer information networks), C-SPAN fits nicely among the high tech media which will likely help to shape the intellectual future of the nation. In some cases, the students reporting on C-SPAN will, for the first time, discover television programming that is actually useful. That can be a real revelation for some of them. What's more, they tend to like it.

The version of the assignment that works best is when C-SPAN happens to be covering something relevant to the genre of the class. Perhaps my greatest success happened several years ago when the group assignment coincided with the Congressional hearings on whether Rural Electrification Associations (REAs) should be allowed to extend cable television to non-metro areas. While preparing their group report, the students learned from C-SPAN and Congress that non-metro areas held slightly more than forty percent of the potential U.S. television audience. They learned that forty percent got its TV fare from three or four broadcast signals and/or a personally owned, "backyard" satellite antenna. And they learned, in minute detail, the competing economic and communicative forces which vied for the attention of the U.S. television audience.

First, my affluent, mostly urban student groups marvelled that forty percent of the U.S. audience *did not* have thirty-channel television. Second, and correctly, they had trouble understanding why cable networks and others had not been more aggressive earlier in efforts to capture that large market. Third, the students could not understand why non-metro audiences failed to rally around the REAs to get "thirty channel TV" for their neighborhoods. They found it hard to understand why the hearings were not discussed on the evening broadcast network news. Finally, they decided that C-SPAN was absolutely essential for our democratic way of life and that there should be several more networks like C-SPAN. Obviously, I had watched the birth of some C-SPAN junkies.

Opportunities to simultaneously study both C-SPAN and its programming are rare. Consequently, I have a second version of the assignment which requires a student group to report on the "primary issue" covered by C-SPAN during a given week and to analyze the personal communication of its participants. This assignment works best in junior/senior level mass communication theory classes and requires some heavy C-SPAN viewing by members of the group. It almost always generates some lively debate about what the "primary issue" was. Usually the groups equate "the most important issue" to "the issue we found most interesting." The number of legislators they recognize—especially those from their state—strongly influences the final decision. I should note that I'm really not concerned with which issue they chose, I only want to encourage them to interact with each other and to spend some time with C-SPAN programming.

The benefits of my "primary issue" assignment are several. First, students learn the technology and design of C-SPAN. They are encouraged to continue their contact with its programming. They usually are amazed by Congressional goings on, especially the visual chaos during regular session and the Special Sessions when legislators speak to an empty chamber. But, they also are impressed by their Representatives' use of argument, by their indifferent reaction to emotionally charged verbiage, and by their long work day. After the group process of organizing and reporting all that within the time frames provided, my students seem always to have discovered how a medium, even one as simple in concept as C-SPAN is, has changed their formerly stereotyped, popular notions about Congress. Some students formulate entirely new attitudes about political communication. Their discoveries and their curiosity generate questions of "Why no C-SPAN-type coverage of the Supreme Court?" and more recently (since C-SPAN 2's demise on our local TCI cable system), "Why not the Senate?" Finally, and of greater importance to my advanced media theory classes, these group report assignments give my students a classical example of an efficient "sense extension" medium; that is, a medium which does little programming other than to extend the viewer's audio/visual perception into a reality which they otherwise would not personally experience. C-SPAN is a good example because, as explained above, it is capable of causing change in their personal attitudes. I should add that not all of my students' discoveries are positive. For example, they love to point out samples of transparent, condescending, wind-bagging, pork barreling or jaw-boning verbiage, especially when it is used by non-congressional persons appearing in sub-committee hearings. At an entirely different level, they often experience considerable dissonance when their attitudes toward their local cable company are juxtaposed with the fact that C-SPAN is sponsored by that company.

On balance, my C-SPAN assignments are exceptional learning experiences. Required study of C-SPAN, the medium, almost always demonstrates that an objective medium can make a difference, not just to "the public at large," but, personally, to each student whose attention is focused, albeit forcibly, on it. My recommendation is to be sure that your students meet C-SPAN personally, not just as a source of material you bring to use in your classes. Then at the end of the term, C-SPAN will be a tool, not just another anonymous class "handout" to be stuffed, sloppily, in the back of their minds.

■ 10
The Media Policy Course

Bruce E. Drushel

Among the challenges for those who teach the Electronic Media Policy course is making the subject matter as accessible as possible to the large number of students for whom it is a major requirement. A wide variety of videotaped material is available to illustrate abstract concepts and to start class discussion. This article outlines topics covered in the typical media policy course for which videotapes from C-SPAN are available, and offers a specific listing of C-SPAN tapes the author has found useful.

Those of us who willingly study and write about media policy too often forget that not everyone, and particularly not every student, shares our interest. To us, the ideas themselves are exciting and engaging; they go to the very heart of the debate over where to strike the balance between social progress and individual rights. To many students, day after day of abstract concepts such as public trustee, intellectual property, and vertical integration is, to be kind, tedious.

Given a group of mature students with a genuine interest in the topic, broad-ranging readings outside of class linked to open seminar-style discussion in class is a good method of adding meaning to that which is ethereal. But the ideal is seldom the reality. Any one of the following conditions dooms a pure discussion format from the start: a media policy course that is a major requirement, course sections that are large, or an undergraduate population that undertakes reading assignments mostly to study for tests.

The challenge for the instructor then becomes making electronic media policy accessible to the masses, or at least, the mass communication major.

There can be little doubt that thought-provoking readings, and stimulating and guided discussion are key components. But we ought also to consider the possibilities for illustrating points through living, breathing, and moving example: videotape.

I had already been using illustrative tape in the media policy course at Miami University before attending C-SPAN in the Classroom's Summer Seminar for Professors. Some of the tape was very good: a "MacNeil-Lehrer Newshour" segment on hate groups on cable access channels, an MTV promotional spot for a contest in which the first prize was to own a radio station, and Geraldo getting his nose broken by a hurled chair. The C-SPAN seminar made me aware of other possibilities: showing the FCC at work in a hearing, and presenting contrasting opinions on issues from people having a stake in those issues.

A Video Syllabus

At Miami University, the broad area of mass communications law is divided between two courses: media law, which focuses on press issues, and electronic media policy, which focuses on regulatory issues in broadcasting, cable, and the "new" media. The electronic media policy course is taught in a small lecture-discussion format. Class sections typically contain 30 students each, many of whom take the course only because it is a major requirement. The class meets for seventy-five minutes twice a week for fifteen weeks.

As one might expect, not all course topics lend themselves to illustration or enhancement using videotape. Among these are the introduction to the course, half of the meetings in a six-meeting unit on Krasnow, Longley, and Terry's (1982) regulatory players, a day spent on legal research sources and techniques, a two-meeting unit on copyright law and its relevance to the electronic media, and a three-meeting unit on ownership and licensing.

But many topics do lend themselves to enhancement using videotape. The following, by topic, represents my attempt to integrate C-SPAN footage and other video into the course.

The Federal Communications Commission

Because of its central role in the development of media policy, the regulatory players unit begins with the FCC. I begin with an explanation of administrative agencies, and move to functions specific to the Commission. Near the end, I play a sample of an FCC hearing (1985), which we discuss briefly. This tape is no longer available, but any discussion of the FCC would be useful for this class.

The Federal Courts

I begin with a discussion of the distinction between evidentiary and appellate proceedings, and use that as a basis for describing the structure of the federal court system. I close with a reference to the radio station format debate (e.g., *FCC v. WNCN Listeners Guild*, 1981) to illustrate the sometimes delicate and contentious relationship between the FCC and the bench, and to introduce a symposium covered by C-SPAN. Video: Federal Courts and the Federal Communications Commission (ID# 598).

The Public

This meeting begins with a discussion of the catalysts of the social activism of the 1960s and moves to the well-known WLBT case (*Office of Communication of the United Church of Christ v. FCC*, 1969), in which citizens groups were first granted standing in station license hearings. It concludes with descriptions of some of the recent notable groups, including Action for Childrens Television, Media Access Project, and the Parents Music Resource Center (PMRC). Video: Untitled PMRC promotional video.

Regulatory Foundations

While it is far more typical to begin a policy course with discussions of the Communications Act of 1934 and the U.S. Constitution, specifically the First Amendment, I have found that delaying them until after the unit on the regulatory players provides a better introduction to current policy issues. Video: The Fairness Doctrine in the Wake of Deregulation (ID# 2577). To illustrate the concept of a public trustee, I use a segment in which the Fairness Doctrine is analyzed for its acceptability as a limitation on the broadcasters' First Amendment rights.

Network Controls

Two class meetings explore the issues that prompted the FCC to regulate indirectly the activities of radio networks in the 1940s and the television networks in the 1970s. C-SPAN coverage of a symposium during which one of the regulations, the Financial Interest and Syndication Rule, was reconsidered contains a colorful presentation by MPAA President Jack Valenti that provides an excellent, if somewhat slanted, summary of the rule. Video: Fin-Syn Debate (ID #8758).

Obscenity and Indecency

Because of the possibilities, both aural and visual, of illustrating controls on offensive content in the electronic media, it is tempting to supplement discussion of those controls with a few too many tapes. In addition to audio excerpts from George Carlin, Howard Stern, and The Greaseman, I use selected segments of one C-SPAN tape that discuss legal approaches to defining indecency and the movie whose nude scene prompted action against a Kansas City television station that aired it uncut. Video: What's Indecent? Who Decides? (ID# 12068); nude scene from *Private Lessons*.

Advertising

I begin by addressing the Federal Trade Commission as another example of administrative agency, and attempt to delineate the jurisdictional boundaries between the FTC and the FCC. A good deal of the meeting is spent on the *Central Hudson* test (*Central Hudson Gas and Electric Corp. v. Public Service Commission of New York*, 1980) and its application to the advertising of controversial products and services. Video: Free Speech and Advertising — Who Draws the Line? (1987). I use a segment in which the application of *Central Hudson* to cigarette advertising is discussed by attorneys representing tobacco companies and public health groups.

Political Broadcasting Rules

Two class meetings are devoted to sections 312 and 315 of the Communications Act, known collectively as the Political Broadcasting Rules. Generally speaking, we spend the first day on the Equal Access provisions, and the second on the Reasonable Access provisions. Video: The Annenberg Washington Program symposium on political broadcasting (ID# 1597). Although the tape is full of good discussion of the relevance of the rules, I particularly favor an exchange between Henry Geller and former FCC Chairman Charles Ferris.

The Fairness Doctrine

Although the main part of the Fairness Doctrine was repealed by the FCC in 1987, I continue to devote two class sessions to it for several reasons. First, since the FCC continues to enforce several of the corollaries, it is necessary to explain their origins, and therefore, the Doctrine itself. Second, because the U.S. Supreme Court's 1969 *Red Lion* opinion relating to the Doctrine is one of the most frequently cited decisions in court cases in the electronic media, the context of the decision should be explained. And finally, the process by which the Doctrine was repealed and the reaction on Capitol Hill to that process serves as an excellent example of the complex relationship among broadcasters, Congress, and the FCC. Video: The Fairness Doctrine in the Wake of Deregulation (ID# 2577). I use a segment in which the panelists speculate on the continued viability of the Fairness Doctrine corollaries.

Cable

The final two class meetings of the semester center on cable, and how government policy has evolved in response to its growth, popularity, and the nature of the services it provides. Video: Three possible C-SPAN videotapes are Telephone Entry into Cable TV Industry (ID# 11344), Cable Television Regulation Act (ID# 14005), and the Future of Cable Television (ID# 13319).

Conclusion

Student reaction to use of the videotape segments has been positive. The principal benefits to the course appear to be in illustrating concepts mentioned in readings and class discussion, stimulating additional discussion, and casting policy issues as matters on which the players described by Krasnow, et al. (1982) have strong opinions.

Video from C-SPAN and other sources has the potential to enliven course topics that, to the average student, otherwise may be less than exciting. But the usual cautionary notes apply: the segments should be brief, economical, and illustrative, and the instructor must be willing to set up the class and afterward discuss what has been seen. Just as a journalist would not use a quotation when a paraphrase would do better, instructors must guard against using video when other methods would be more effective.

References

Videotapes:
Cable television regulation act. (1990, September 10). ID# 14005.
Fairness Doctrine in the wake of deregulation. (1988, April 5). ID# 2577.
Federal courts & the Federal Communications Commission. (1988, January 20). ID# 598.
Fin-Syn debate. (1989, June 5). ID# 8758.
Future of cable television. (1990, July 27). ID# 13319.
Telephone entry into cable TV industry. (1990, February 26). ID# 11344.
What's indecent? Who decides? (1990, April 18). ID# 12068.
Political broadcasting rules (1987, October). Annenberg Washington program panel discussion. ID# 1597.
Short Subjects (various titles and dates). *C-SPAN in the Classroom.* Available individually or in compilation form.
Parents' Music Resource Center. Untitled promotional videotape.
Other sources:
Free speech and advertising—Who draws the line? (1987, April). Boston, MA: Institute for Democratic Communication, Boston University.

Central Hudson Gas & Electric Corp. v. Public Service Commission of New York, 447 U.S. 557 (1980).

Federal Communications Commission v. WNCN Listeners Guild, 450 U.S. 582 (1981).

Krasnow, E. G., Longley, L. D., & Terry, H. A. (1982). *The politics of broadcast regulation, 3rd. ed.* New York, NY: St. Martin's Press.

Office of Communication of the United Church of Christ, et al. v. Federal Communications Commission, 359 F.2d 994 (1969).

Red Lion Broadcasting Co. v. Federal Communications Commission, 395 U.S. 367 (1969).

■ 11

The Broadcast Journalism Course

Robert J. Snyder

C-SPAN can help broadcast journalism professors achieve numerous pedagogical goals. This chapter discusses how using a speech by Linda Ellerbee, presented on C-SPAN, allows students to put reporting concepts and theories into practice. Further discussion exposes students to some of the limitations of journalism.

C-SPAN is an excellent teaching tool for getting broadcast journalism students to put into practice course content and theory. My goal in teaching broadcast news is that first, students should be able to use media appropriately; second, students should be exposed to the "reality" of working in media; and third, students should also develop a better understanding of what is news. Additionally, one problem with teaching broadcast news is that often times giving students real-life reporting assignments can be difficult. Assign students to cover an on-campus event and one or more of them has a conflict and cannot do it. Or worse yet, I am at the point in my reporting class where students are ready to start covering events and nothing is happening in the area. C-SPAN is a useful solution to these problems. Pre-taped events for classroom use removes student conflicts and provides an event when no other is available. I find that C-SPAN is most useful for beginning reporting classes. Students start to get a feel for staying with events and then having to sift through the coverage and determine what is newsworthy.

Speeches are good events to use. In many ways they are simple events to cover. In its simplest form, a reporter sits through a speech and tries to make stories out of the person's main points. The event itself is news. I use a C-SPAN speech for the first real reporting assignment in my Radio

News Course. Students enrolled in this class have already taken Broadcast News Writing and ideally are mastering broadcast news style. Introducing audio as a story telling tool is the next logical step.

Prior to covering the speech, lectures are given on how to use, select and write to sound bites. For example, bites are often twenty seconds or less (much to the consternation of many newsmakers) and lead-in sentences to sound bites should not "echo" the sound bite. Students are then given the speech assignment to put into practice the concepts they have just learned. Like any good reporter, students must do some research beforehand to learn what they can about the speaker and topic. Then students sit through C-SPAN coverage of a speech.

Students are to produce two readers of forty-five seconds in length or less, using two different sound bites. Based on the short-length and number of daily radio newscasts, most radio stations produce at least two different versions of stories.

For this assignment, I use a speech by commentator and now-television producer Linda Ellerbee. Ellerbee spoke to a conference on Men, Women and Media on April 10, 1989 (ID# 7088). Students listen to the entire event, including the introduction and the question-and-answer session. The instructor can have the option of making the assignment due at the end of class and simulate deadlines, or due at the start of the next class, especially if this is a first reporting assignment. I prefer to have the stories due at the start of the next class so students have as much time as possible to prepare good work. Assignments with deadlines can be made at any time. To start, I'd rather have students really think through and apply the concepts discussed in class. Either way, students get experience working with and writing to sound bites based on a real event.

When I grade the stories, I look for execution of concepts. Is the script in the correct format? Is the sound bite set up well? Does the story make sense, etc. After the stories are evaluated, I set aside one session for discussion of the stories and events. Students are provided with examples of their peers' work (with the names removed) to see how well students have applied the concepts. I try to find "good" and "weak" stories.

Based on past experience, students learn a number of additional things when they discuss their stories besides so-called mistakes in execution of the style, format and concepts already presented in class. For example, students learn that what is newsworthy to one reporter is not necessarily news to another reporter. If there are nine students in the class, it is very possible that there may be eighteen different stories or versions of this event. It has happened before in my class. This, in turn, leads into a discussion on what is news and the limitations of broadcast news as a source of information.

What I have found most fascinating in this assignment is the selection of sound bites for the stories. There generally is a clear distinction between the sound bites women in the class choose and sound bites men choose. Ellerbee is a great speaker and the students generally enjoy her speech. During her speech, Ellerbee defines feminism. To Ellerbee, feminism means "equality between men and women. . . that's all it means. And if you believe that, you're a feminist." So, according to Ellerbee anybody can be a feminist.

Perhaps not so surprising, women generally pick that excerpt for a sound bite. The men generally do not. However, the men often pick up on one of Ellerbee's main points that while women have made progress in the area of salaries, women still lack any real positions of power in major media. In follow up discussion, I ask my students why do they think women select the feminism message but not the men? The class generally agrees that perhaps the men just can't relate to feminism since feminism is a "woman's topic."

That may very well be. It is at that point I distribute a handout from Shoemaker and Reese's (1991) *Mediating the Message, Theories of Influences on Mass Media Content* (p. 55). The authors argue that while as journalists we are to follow the ideal of objectivity, we are in fact unique human beings who bring a baggage of personal experience to the stories they cover. I explain to my students that this exercise suggests that it is very difficult to set that baggage aside. Now that says a lot about what is considered news—something most of my students have never even thought about before.

C-SPAN coverage of speeches is but one example instructors can use. C-SPAN provides regular coverage of National Press Club Speeches which make for useful events to cover. Numerous congressional hearings are carried on C-SPAN. Again, research before the event can play a role in the assignment. For example, TV news courses can produce stories by editing C-SPAN coverage. The opportunities for putting C-SPAN to use in reporting courses are endless and can accomplish numerous educational goals as the previous example should demonstrate.

Certainly using C-SPAN should not replace those "out of classroom" experiences. C-SPAN seems most effective in beginning courses where students can be introduced to such concepts as selecting and writing to sound bites, but can also accomplish additional pedagogical goals such as giving students a better understanding of the limitations of journalism.

References

Ellerbee, L. (1989, April 10). And so it goes. (ID# 7088).

Shoemaker, P. J. and Reese, S. D. (1991). *Mediating the message. Theories of influences on mass media content.* White Plains, NY: Longman Publishing.

■ 12

Gate Keeping and Agenda-Setting

Rod Carveth

This essay reviews the use of C-SPAN as a tool to teach the concepts of gatekeeping and agenda-setting in mass communication classes. For a class assignment in a broadcast news and public affairs class, students were instructed to watch the Anita Hill-Clarence Thomas hearings on C-SPAN, and compare the live coverage of the hearings with network news stories of them. As a result of this exercise, students were able to see how what they saw on C-SPAN differed what they saw on the network news. An indirect benefit of this exercise was the heightening of student awareness of the issue of sexual harassment. Other methods of integrating C-SPAN into broadcast news classes are discussed.

Two important concepts in broadcast news are gatekeeping and agenda-setting. Gatekeeping refers to the editorial process of selecting events and components of events for news coverage. Agenda-setting can be considered to be the outcome of the process of gatekeeping. The selection of news events represents the news "agenda" for the day. Research by McCombs and Shaw (1972) has demonstrated that what the news audience considers to be important public issues correlates highly with the issues presented in the news. Thus, it is argued, the news media help set the agenda for what the public considers to be important issues of the day.

While lecturing about gatekeeping and agenda-setting is one method of presenting these concepts to students, other methods can be used in broadcast news and journalism classes to help students understand these two very important concepts. One method I have tried is to assign students to write a story about an event that is happening at the university or in the community, and then compare their stories with those that appear in the local media. There are two drawbacks to this exercise. First, since many of the assignments involve covering preplanned, scheduled events (such as campus speakers), assigning students to cover an event does not necessarily mean that the event will get covered by the local media. Thus, there is nothing to compare their stories to. Second, while one consistent source of coverage is the campus weekly newspaper, its level of professionalism and quality of writing is virtually indistinguishable from that of my students. Hence, the impact of the assignment is lost.

Another alternative is to have students cover breaking stories. The drawback is finding breaking stories that interest students. In fact, during twelve years of teaching, I have been dismayed by students' lack of awareness of public affairs in general. Many students are politically apathetic and largely ignorant about the legislative process. For many, the only issues that are relevant are those that happen to them personally.[1]

This problem was magnified while I was teaching at the University of Hartford. Many students were from other states, and did not have knowledge of, or interest in, issues such as the state income tax debate, or recycling legislation. I usually gave a "current events" quiz in such classes to determine student awareness about contemporary events. The majority of students could not name a Congressperson, a U.S. senator from Connecticut, or senators from their respective states.

During the summer of 1991, I attended the C-SPAN Seminar for Professors. I attended the seminar because I wanted to use C-SPAN to help educate my students not only about news, but also about politics and government. I especially wanted to discover ways to integrate C-SPAN coverage of Congressional debates, hearings and press conferences in my news courses. One example presented during the seminar was particularly intriguing: compare C-SPAN coverage of a hearing with the network news

---

1   For example, in the spring of 1991, while I was at the university of Hartford, an event occurred which held a high degree of personal salience for my students. A riot broke out on campus following an after-hours altercation between students and campus police. Eventually several hundred students joined in the melee, and police from surrounding communities (Hartford, West Hartford and Bloomfield) were called in to keep the peace. Unfortunately, passions rose, fourteen students were arrested, and there were several allegations of police brutality. The story received headline coverage in all the print and broadcast media, and continued for ten days. The story would not have received such intensive coverage except for the fact that several students had videotaped the riot. The tapes, which revealed instances of police brutality, and followed just days after the Rodney King incident in Los Angeles, were used extensively by the local TV stations. Students were quite eager to talk about the riot in my "Discovering the News" class. Not surprisingly, there were almost as many versions of what happened as there were students. A protest rally was held following the riot. My students were assigned to cover the event, and bring their stories to class for discussion. We then compared local media coverage to student coverage. The exercise vividly demonstrated issues of gatekeeping and agenda-setting.

coverage of that hearing. Questions to be raised for class include: What portions of the hearing made the news? Which members of Congress, government officials, and witnesses received coverage? Were excerpts from the debate taken out of context? This exercise held a great deal of potential for not only raising the level of awareness about news coverage among my students, but also raising their awareness about politics and government. After the seminar, I decided to try this exercise in my class.

What eventually happened was a combination of planning and luck. During the fall semester, I taught a course in broadcast news and public affairs. Forty students were enrolled in the course. I had planned to spend three to four weeks lecturing about broadcast news and the government. C-SPAN was to play an integral role.

During the first day of class, I asked students if they had ever watched C-SPAN. Only one student had watched the network, and that was merely out of curiosity. (He said he was flipping through the dial and came upon the channel accidently. The confirmation hearings for Judge David Souter were on and he watched for about fifteen minutes.) Six students could identify the channel. For the majority of students, C-SPAN was to be a brand new experience.

Fortunately for the class, cable TV had just been installed on campus. Most students lived on campus and would not have been able to receive C-SPAN otherwise.

I originally assigned students to compare C-SPAN coverage of the Senate Judiciary Committee hearings on Supreme Court nominee Clarence Thomas to the network news coverage of the hearings. Unfortunately, the confirmation hearings held little actual news value beyond the first day, and students, by and large, were not especially interested in the confirmation process. The network's coverage of the hearings lacked a strong news peg, so it was not surprising that the students had a difficult time comparing the two. I did demonstrate to them, through a review of C-SPAN's coverage of the hearings, that the networks were trying to drum up drama where there was very little. For example, I compared an exchange between Judge Thomas and Senator Howard Metzenbaum that was rather tame on C-SPAN, but when edited by ABC looked dramatic.

No one (myself included) expected the last minute allegations that Supreme Court nominee Clarence Thomas had sexually harassed law professor Anita Hill while she was at the Department of Education and, later, the Equal Employment Opportunity Commission. The rather colorless confirmation process took a dramatic and bizarre turn with this story. It also provided me with another opportunity to compare broadcast network and C-SPAN coverage.

I next assigned students to watch a minimum of six hours of C-SPAN coverage of the Thomas-Hill hearings, and to watch a minimum of three network nightly newscasts over the weekend. They were to write a three to five page paper comparing the two and to be prepared for class discussion.

Student Reactions

There was a much more positive response with this exercise. First, Professor Hill's allegations of sexual harassment by Judge Thomas piqued student interest. As a result, they became more involved in the assignment. Many students reported that they were "riveted" to their TV sets during the weekend. One student reported she could not "believe that I watched about twelve hours of this stuff."

Second, many students saw networks attempt to make a contest out of the hearings. A majority of students commented that all the networks brought in experts to comment on who was ahead and who was behind during the hearings. One student commented "It was like a boxing match, and the commentators were scoring rounds." Another student compared the hearing more to professional wrestling because "it's all set up in advance." About a dozen students reported that watching the hearings on the networks was like being on a roller coaster . . . one minute Hill is up, then Thomas." Finally, one student commented, "The only thing missing was little 'Bud' and 'Bud Light' bottles in a hearing room accusing each other on topics of tasting great and being less filling."

More importantly, students noted the process of gatekeeping at work. For example, the majority of students noted that the networks focused on the most extreme elements of the Senate Judiciary Committee investigation, such as "Long Dong Silver," a movie Judge Thomas allegedly revealed to Professor Hill that he had seen. By contrast, many students noted that the networks did not do a good job of giving viewers, as one student noted, "a feel of the hearings." For example, eight students observed that network TV news stories of Judge Thomas' opening statement to the Senate Judiciary Committee lacked the dramatic impact of watching it live on C-SPAN. By contrast, fifteen students reported in their papers that network stories failed to convey the repetitiveness of the questioning. "A lot of the questions covered the same thing," one student reported. "It got kinda boring." Another student commented "The exchanges between Hill or Thomas and the senator for the moment were for the most part long, ragged dialogues that resembled those of the senator previous. However, turn on the evening news and you are treated to sequences of intense questioning by well-prepared senators moving in for the kill, and poetic answers by the emotional Hill and Thomas."

All the students noted how this incident was one of the few times that network TV had dealt with sexual harassment. Students wondered why the topic had received so little attention, and why networks and newspapers alike began to devote so much time and space to the issue. We discussed how this dramatic incident moved sexual harassment up on the media agenda. I asked students in my class whether their friends were discussing sexual harassment. Everyone reported yes. That revelation brought home vividly the notion of agenda-setting.

The topic of sexual harassment also made for some lively classroom debate. The class was virtually split down the middle in terms of who they sided with in the debate. This split did not occur along gender lines. Equal numbers of male and female students supported either Thomas or Hill. While not directly part of a class in broadcast news and public affairs, we did discuss the issue of sexual harassment beyond the Hill-Thomas controversy. The sharing of perceptions about what constitutes sexual harassment became an indirect benefit of the exercise.

The only negative aspect of this exercise was that several students noted how disillusioned they were with the government. In particular, they commented on how ineffectual the senators were in their questioning. One student observed that there should be "a Senate Judiciary Committee for the Senate Judiciary Committee." These observations led us to discuss the political nature of the hearings.

Other Applications

C-SPAN coverage of the Hill-Thomas hearings can be used in other ways. For example, later in the semester we discussed how television news is structured as narrative. Topics such as reporters' formulas (Campbell, 1987) and the discursive approach[2] to analyzing television were discussed. Students were shown how the network news stories could be viewed as "mini-dramas," with the "characters" of Anita Hill and Clarence Thomas functioning as symbols for larger societal issues related to race and gender.

The tapes of the Hill-Thomas hearings could also be used for classes in broadcast journalism. For example, students could watch the tapes, and then be assigned to write radio or TV news stories about them. For schools with television editing facilities, they could actually put together news packages. Students could compare their stories with one another, and with actual network news stories.

---

2   The discursive approach to television proposes that TV characters function within a series of textual and intertextual relations. See Fiske, 1987.

Conclusion

There were multiple positive outcomes to this exercise. Beyond introducing the majority of students to C-SPAN, the exercise brought home issues of gatekeeping and agenda-setting. For the students in my broadcast news and public affairs class, the concepts of gatekeeping and agenda-setting came alive for them.

Not all incidents covered on C-SPAN will have the drama of the Hill-Thomas hearings. However, there is enough of a menu of C-SPAN items to select from. For example, C-SPAN often covers the news conferences following major Supreme Court rulings, such as those on abortion.[3] Students could compare what they saw from the C-SPAN coverage of news conferences by "pro-choice" and "pro-life" groups to coverage by network or local news.

C-SPAN's "Road to the White House" series on the 1992 Presidential campaign provides a plethora of live and taped political events useful for a number of classes. In talking about agenda-setting in my mass communication theories class at the University of South Dakota, we compared C-SPAN coverage of the South Dakota Democratic party debate to subsequent network news coverage. We also discussed the lack of coverage of minority candidates. None of the students had heard of the candidates featured in C-SPAN coverage of a March 1992 minority candidates' debate. In that way, we were able to discuss more fully how the media help set the public agenda—telling us who and what is important through what they cover, and who or what is unimportant by their lack of coverage.

Using C-SPAN requires careful planning by the instructor and a few resources, such as tapes and a VCR. Instructors planning to use C-SPAN in the classroom would be well-advised to contact C-SPAN to obtain instructional materials. if department budgets allow, instructors may wish to rent or purchase tapes from the Purdue Video Archives.[4] Finally, instructors should consider attending C-SPAN's Seminar for Professors. Based on my experience, I would recommend that other instructors of news and public affairs consider integrating C-SPAN into their curriculum.

---

3 For example, in 1992 the Supreme Court is scheduled to rule on the constitutionality of the Pennsylvania law restricting abortions.

4 Similarly, network news coverage can be obtained by contacting the Vanderbilt News Archives at Vanderbilt University.

References

Campbell, R. (1987). Securing the middle ground: Reporter formulas in *60 Minutes*. *Critical Studies in Mass Communication, 4,* 325-350.

Fiske, J. (1987)*Television Culture*. London: Methuen.

McCombs, M. & Shaw, D. (1972). The agenda-setting function of mass media. *Public Opinion Quarterly, 36,* 175-187.

☐ Part IV
Crafting Research

■ 13
C-SPAN as a Database for Intercultural Communication

Jim Schnell

*This essay describes methodology used to analyze reaction in the U.S.
to the Chinese pro-democracy movement. Analysis is based on tapes
obtained from the C-SPAN network. Programs were primarily interpreted according to high context/low context messaging evidenced in
the tapes. Application of findings from this analysis can benefit student
understanding in a variety of courses in communication, such as Mass
Media, Persuasion, Cross-Cultural Communication, Rhetorical Communication Theory, Interpersonal Communication, and Public Speaking.*

In recent years the academic community has recognized C-SPAN as a
valuable teaching tool in the classroom. This chapter describes how C-
SPAN can be used for communication-oriented research. Discussion of
this undertaking emphasizes methodology, thus enabling readers to realize possible applications in their own research areas. The primary method
stresses a descriptive analysis of C-SPAN tapes obtained from the Public
Affairs Video Archives at Purdue University.

Within my research area, cross-cultural issues related to U.S.-China
relations, I have focused on reaction in the U.S. to the Chinese pro-

democracy movement using C-SPAN as a representative forum for discussion on the issue. The types of programs analyzed are described later in this chapter.

A selection of programs dealing with reforms in China was obtained from the Public Affairs Video Archives at Purdue University, which provided an annotated list of eighty-two programs (ranging in time from thirty minutes to ten hours and ranging in cost from $30 to $275).

Twenty-two programs were selected based on their relevance to the Chinese pro-democracy movement. Types of programs included forums, news conferences, speeches to the National Press Club, roundtables, speeches, House Committees, call-in shows, House Highlights, Congressional News Conferences, Senate Committees, and book reviews. Several programs are listed in the bibliography. The more relevant programs are noted in the discussion of classroom applications.

Based on observed consistencies, the tapes were coded for high context/low context messaging structures. This type of analysis focuses on the relationship between high context channels of communication used by Chinese speakers, and low context channels of communication used by Americans. For example, Chinese speakers typically use high context channels of communication that tend to be less direct and heavily reliant on nonverbal messages. Meaning evolves from context. American speakers typically use low context channels of communication that tend to be more direct and based on literal verbal statements. One can more easily understand the intended meaning without considering the context.

This illustrates a standard cross-cultural communication dynamic. Cross-cultural misunderstanding can easily occur when interactants use different channels on the high context-low context continuum. Analysis focused on statements by President Bush, U.S. political representatives, Chinese students studying in the U.S., Chinese diplomatic representatives, and the American public. Analysis of these statements consistently reveals the Chinese preference for high context messages and the U.S. preference for low context messages.

The following situation exemplifies the importance of context when analyzing Chinese communication. During the period of June 1-7, 1989 (the Tienanmen Square shootings occurred on June 3) there was much confusion regarding who was in control of the Chinese government and what their position would be toward political and economic reform in China. There were rumors that Chinese leader Deng Xiaopeng was dead and civil war was imminent. American politicians frequently made direct statements in support of the pro-democracy movement and called for the Chinese government to allow reform. The C-SPAN program "China Debate" (ID# 8123) includes such low context messages. The Chinese government released no statements to clarify the situation. However, when Chinese Premier Li Peng (a conservative hard-liner) appeared on Chinese national television wearing a "Chairman Mao uniform" instead of the more common western business suit, viewers could easily interpret the government's position. The context (what he was wearing) spoke far louder than what he was doing (performing ceremonial protocol). The "Chairman Mao uniform" was popular during the conservative reign of Chairman Mao Tse Tung. The fact Premier Li Peng appeared on Chinese national television wearing such clothing indicated he was in charge and that he was a conservative leader. Nothing needed to be stated. In a low context culture such as the United States, we would expect our leader to state his or her position rather than to have to interpret intentions based on clothing.

Findings from this analysis can benefit student understanding in a variety of courses in communication including Mass Media, Persuasion, Cross-Cultural Communication, Rhetorical Communication Theory, Interpersonal Communication, and Public Speaking. This can be done by stressing examples of pertinent course concepts evidenced in the C-SPAN tapes.

In the Persuasion course, I emphasize the importance of diplomatic dialogue between nations, especially when the nations are in disagreement. The C-SPAN program "Bush Policy Toward China" (ID# 10260) describes National Security Advisor Brent Scowcroft's trip to China and President Bush's policy of maintaining dialogue. This situation illuminates the relevance of diplomatic dialogue and it exemplifies high context rapport. In the Mass Media course, I emphasize the goal of objectivity stressed by news organizations. The C-SPAN program "China" (ID# 11386) featured Mortimer Zuckerman (Editor-in-Chief of *U.S. News and World Report*) discussing the 1989 cover story "Inside China: The First Interviews with China's Leaders Since Tienanmen Square." His discussion clarifies the concern with objectivity, accuracy, and journalistic resourcefulness. It also exemplifies the role of U.S. media when they translate high context messages from Chinese leaders into low context meanings sought by the American audience.

In the Cross-Cultural Communication course, the influence of societal frames of reference are emphasized. China is a socialist nation and the U.S. is capitalist. The C-SPAN program "Sino-U.S. Relations" (ID# 2090) features a speech by Chinese Foreign Minister Wu Xuequian. His speech describes China's reforming economy and it's opening to the outside world. His subject exemplifies the difficulty of two systems, which have differing societal frames of reference, and are unable to find common ground. The high context messages of intention enhance this process.

What applies at the international level frequently applies at the interpersonal level.

There are many who argue scholarly research is done at the expense of time that can be put toward effective teaching. Use of C-SPAN in the aforementioned manner allows the faculty member to meet both objectives competently. Analysis of C-SPAN programming enables the professor to pursue significant scholarly research. As described in this chapter, such scholarly research has relevance for both teaching and research.

References

Bush policy toward China (1989, December 12). Call In. ID# 10260.
China (1990, March 6). Call In. ID# 11386.
China debate (1989, June 22). House highlight. ID# 8123.
Sino-U.S. relations (1988, March 9). National press club speech. ID# 2090.

■ 14

Congressman James A. Traficant, Jr.: A Critical Analysis

Kathleen M. Golden

This study examines the ideology of Congressman James A. Traficant, Jr., a Democrat representing the 17th Congressional District in Ohio. Using one minute speeches and call in shows featured on C-SPAN, this chapter examines Traficant's discourse on taxes, foreign trade, Israel, and the IRS. The unedited segments aired on C-SPAN reveal significant rhetorical aspects worthy of examination from an ideological perspective.

Sillars (1991) closes his book on communication criticism with a chapter on ideological criticism. He observes that ideological criticism carries us to the point of recognizing good reasons for engaging in right action, situating what is "good and right" in an historical context, and understanding efforts of real people to create a better world (p. 207). This ideological focus serves as a good starting point for this critical analysis.

There is little attempt to deny a political bias in ideological criticism. This becomes doubly confusing when one is dealing with a political figure. There is a distinct relationship between the rhetor and critic in ideological criticism due to the involved analysis of both the rhetor and his or her political and social milieu. The job for one looking at ideology, and the power associated with it, is to attempt to pare through the "surface structure" arguments and see the "deep structure" that houses the underlying reasons and historical bases of those arguments.

Criticism of the historical situations surrounding the rhetoric of a political figure is vital to the understanding of ideology. When examining the rhetoric of a politician, one should look at both what the figure says, but also at what others say about him or her. There are some distinct problems in discovering information about politicians, primarily because of the way political news is disseminated, that is by the leader or his or her staff. This presents a problem, since most officials are hesitant to include negative information in their press releases. This is where C-SPAN becomes a valuable research tool. C-SPAN provides unedited comments from the two Congressional floors, unlike the transcripts provided in the *Congressional Record*, which can be changed, deleted, or corrected. Many times this change will be grammatical, but sometimes it involves substantive modifications of what has been heard on the floor of Congress.

Letters to the editor in local newspapers are often helpful in determining the acceptance or rejection of a particular politician and his or her ideology. Voting records for elections for that political office can often show support by constituents. Articles run in local newspapers in the political official's constituency also add insight. These sources, and C-SPAN's coverage, provide useful material for evaluating James A. Traficant, Jr., and public reaction to his rhetoric.

Data

Traficant was chosen for study because he has gained a great deal of media exposure during the last few years. In 1990, he appeared twice on the "Donahue" show and once with Morley Safer on CBS's "60 Minutes." He is also regularly featured on C-SPAN. He appears on call in programs, and he exercises his Congressional privilege speaking for one minute each day before the sessions begin. These speeches known as "One Minutes" are broadcast on C-SPAN to all homes which carry this cable service.

Transcripts of major network broadcasts can be obtained from Journal Graphics, a transcription house for these programs. Some C-SPAN transcripts are available through the Purdue Archives, others can be developed by listening to the videotapes of broadcasts and then correcting the *Congressional Record* to match what actually occurred on the floor.

According to a review of the *Congressional Record Index* for January 1990-February 1992, Traficant spends most of his time on the Congressional floor discussing four major issues. These issues include Israel, taxes, foreign trade, and the IRS. Many of his one minute speeches deal with two or three of these issues at a time. For this study, concentration will focus on the C-SPAN call-in programs, one minute speeches from the House floor, and debate regarding the four major subjects. The *Congressional Record Index* provides information on the appearances by Traficant, the Purdue Archives provides a database search of ninety-five one minute speeches delivered in 1990 and the videotapes of viewer call in shows broadcast on C-SPAN.

It is the contention of many qualitative researchers, that triangulation is a vital part of research. This can involve the use of multiple sources of data or methods. Questions of reliability are enhanced through data triangulation. Historical context also becomes important in the analysis.

Historical Context

James A. Traficant, Jr. was the sheriff of Mahoning County, of which Youngstown is the county seat. He earned a B.S. at the University of Pittsburgh and a M.S. at Youngstown State University. He gained most of his notoriety for his involvement in a racketeering trial in the early 1980s where he was charged with taking a political contribution from mob bosses, the Carrabia brothers. Even though he was not an attorney, he defended himself in district court and was found not guilty in June, 1983. He became a local hero. Interestingly, he later was charged in tax court, was found guilty of tax evasion, and is currently paying over $180,000 in back taxes and penalties.

Youngstown is a community that was devastated by three steel mill closings in the late 1970s and early 1980s. The economic base of the community had been steel and once that was decimated, community members were jobless and looking for leadership. James Traficant turned from being sheriff to a run for Congress in 1984. He won the 17th Congressional District seat by defeating the incumbent Lyle Williams by 17,565 votes ("Traficant vote," 1988, Nov. 15, 1). His victory over the Republican challengers in each election has been greater than the one before (1).

In an ongoing study of network news appearances of members of Congress, Foote (1991) released his report on the 101st Congress (1989-90). For the first time the House of Representatives outdistanced the Senate in network news appearances. A new generation of congressmen and women grew up with TV and consciously used it to build credibility and power in Washington (1). Not surprisingly, Foote says, it was Gingrich who took best advantage of televised coverage of the House when cameras made their first appearances there in 1979. At the end of the day, he made speeches to an empty chamber—but also to a respectable national television audience on C-SPAN (1-2).

Traficant had only one network news appearance during his first term in office (1985-86). That jumped to fourteen in 1987-88 and the latest figures on the 1989-90 term show him having nine appearances. He was second in Ohio for Representatives in 1987-88 and third in Ohio for Representatives in 1989-90. The first place Representative received the most coverage due to a sex scandal which cost him his re-election bid in 1990.

Traficant was launched into the national limelight by getting air time on television news programs precisely because of the C-SPAN coverage. Traficant's first major media coverage came during his floor debate over a measure to impose a moratorium on aid to contra rebels in Nicaragua. He said,

> The president sees the contra leadership as freedom fighters and heroes. I do not mean to be sarcastic, but I see them as sort of like the Three Stooges of Central America. I do not mean Moe, Larry, and Curley. I mean Robelo, Cruz, and Calero . . . . In fact, to me it looks like a domestic dispute now, and I sort of liken the president to a piano player in a house of ill repute. When the sheriff raids it, he says, "I really didn't know what was going on. I was just playing the piano." (De Souza, 1987, A1, A10)

This marked the beginning of the media's use of sound bites from Traficant's speeches. Traficant's office claimed to have received thirty letters based on his speech including requests for interviews by magazines and newspapers as well as the Christian Broadcasting Network (De Souza, 1987, A1).

In Morley Safer's "60 Minutes" program on Traficant, he said "virtually none of Traficant's fellow Congressmen would comment on the record on their colleague from Youngstown" (1990, November 11). In the same segment from "60 Minutes," mention was made of Traficant's involvement in two alleged Nazi war criminal cases. Traficant was asked by the family of John Demjanjuk to look into the charges that Demjanjuk gassed 850,000 Jews in Treblinka. Traficant's involvement in this case drew the attention of Arthur Rudolph supporters. They believe the ex-NASA rocket scientist was forced, by officials from Office of Special Investigations (OSI), to sign a confession that he was a Nazi officer.

Due to his connections with the cases of John J. Demjanjuk and Arthur Rudolph, Traficant was invited to attend a 1988 Populist Party national committee meeting held in Cincinnati, Ohio. The Anti-Defamation League labels the Populist Party an "extremist mix of former members of the Ku Klux Klan, neo-Nazis, followers of Lyndon LaRouche and Posse Comitatus . . . , an Anti-Semitic paramilitary group" (De Souza, 1987, 1). A letter to the editor in the Youngstown newspaper, the *Vindicator*, written by two professors from Youngstown State University and the secretary of the Zionist Organization of America, was addressed to Traficant. It demanded an explanation for his appearance at the Populist Party meeting. They chided Traficant for his behavior,

> Traficant saluted the Populists, saying, "I think you've got something good going here." Then, obviously ignorant of the racists [sic], nativist sentiments

of the movement, he called Populism generally and the Populist party specifically the wave of the future.... Congressman Traficant owes the voters of this district—men an [sic] women, black and white, ethnic and immigrant—explanations: for his embarrassing involvement with the Populists, for his equally embarrassing involvement in the Demjanjuk and Rudolph cases and his one minute tirades on the floor of the U.S. Congress. (Spiegel, Friedman & Kutler, 1990, p. 16)

Accusations of Traficant's anti-semitism are tied to two factors. One is his defense of two accused Nazi war criminals: Arthur Rudolph and John Demjanjuk. The second is his open criticism of the American Israeli Public Affairs Committee (AIPAC) and his lack of support for foreign aid to Israel.

Traficant provides documentation from the Demjanjuk investigation to be printed in the *Congressional Record* (1991, March 1, E735-E737; 1991, March 6, E793-E795). The investigation, spearheaded by Traficant, has stirred much controversy. New evidence has been uncovered that Demjanjuk has been mistaken for "Ivan the Terrible." In his one minute speech, Traficant says,

> Mr. Speaker, CBS's crew of "Sixty Minutes" flew to Poland. They heard of a woman who said she had known of Ivan the Terrible. Maria Dudek, 70 years old, told Ed Bradley off camera that she knew Ivan well. He would take gold from the Jewish prisoners and come to town. He would buy vodka from her husband and pay for the right and privilege to sleep with her. Also, Mr. Speaker, Maria Dudek said she knew this man by his real family's name, Ivan Marczenko. Ivan Marczenko's name is listed under the Polish War Crimes Committee as being a known Ukrainian guard at Treblinka. John Demjanjuk was convicted of this crime; his name appears on no list anywhere in the world.... (*Congressional Record*, 1990, February 28, H518)

This case has become a mission for Traficant. His past dealings with the tax court have made him suspicious of many government investigative branches; the OSI is but one of them.

Secondly, Traficant's criticism of the AIPAC comes from his attempts to trim the foreign aid budgets. His agenda is to cut foreign aid and put the money into American programs. He says,

> Mr. Speaker, Israel wants ten billion, and what Israel wants Israel usually gets in this body. In fact, it appears to me that Israel has more clout in Washington than California and New York combined. That must be because Los Angeles and New York are in deep trouble . . . . (*Congressional Record*, 1991, September 11, H6393)

On C-SPAN's call-in program (ID# 14456), a caller supports Traficant's stand: "We give too much money to Israel . . . ." Traficant replies, "I am number one on the hit list by the American Israeli Lobby." He goes on to discuss how the collectivity of lobbyists and the Congress makes something happen that would not otherwise. He suggests that the Congress vote with its heart, instead of succumbing to special interest groups.

Related to his disenchantment with the AIPAC and American spending on Israel is his general disgust with our foreign trade policy. Traficant is well-known for his "Buy American" amendments attached to assorted bills coming through Congress. In fact, a "Buy American" amendment was introduced on the House floor by Traficant June 20, 25, 26, and July 18, 1991. Some House members debated the relevance or necessity of such an amendment, but in all four cases it was approved.

Traficant has also been guilty of Japan bashing. This likely prompted C-SPAN to involve Traficant in the first U.S./Japanese Simulcast from Japan (ID# 15166). Traficant states, "I think it's time Americans start taking care of Americans first . . . America can't continue to be the big flea market of the world with an open door for Japan." Many of the same issues are discussed in his one minute speech,

> Mr. Speaker, the controversial Japanese politician Shintaro Isihara, who wrote the book *The Japan That Can Say "No"*, was in America yesterday speaking to a group of workers in Michigan. He said in the past that Americans were lazy and in fact we were racist, and that was our major problem . . . . I say, Mr. Speaker, it is time for a shotgun wedding if Japan does not open up those markets. Our people are losing their jobs, losing their homes, and Japanese politicians are admitting they are practicing illegal trade in closing their markets. Congress ought to be ashamed of themselves. It is time to tell the Japanese we need a new two lane bridge, and we are not going to pay for the bridge this time, and we sure as hell are not going to have a toll road either. (*Congressional Record*, 1991, May 21, H2495)

These arguments are consistent with what Traficant terms the non-existent foreign trade policy. He constantly reiterates that, according to the Constitution, "it is Congress's job to regulate commerce with foreign nations" (ID# 12106).

Traficant often shifts to a discussion of his attitude on taxes, including a plan he has developed called the "50/50 and 5." This is a tax plan which would not raise taxes on the middle class or the poor, but would take the total amount of revenue needed: "50% from NATO, 50% from foreign aid, and 5% from the very wealthy" (ID# 12106).

Traficant's attitude toward taxes is twofold. On one side he thinks that the American people are being taxed to death and on the other hand he is critical of the agents who tax the public, both the Congress and the IRS. Historically, Traficant has had little love for the IRS. He is now paying the back taxes and penalties associated with his own tax evasion case. Traficant takes issue with the IRS on many occasions. In a one minute speech, he argues that the little guy has been getting a raw deal for years. The big guy usually is not hassled, is not audited. When they are, Members, they settle for pennies on the dollars. I think the IRS has become too powerful. Everybody in America knows it. (*Congressional Record*, 1991, March 20, H1852)

His complaints are with the auditing process and the reversal of the burden of proof.

Mr. Speaker, I have never heard so many politicians say that Judge Thomas should get the benefit of the doubt, because in America you are innocent until proven guilty . . . . Now, I agree with that, but the hypocrisy is an American taxpayer is guilty and must prove themselves innocent. Where are all the politicians on this grave and most important constitutional issue? The politicians are hiding . . . . Are they afraid of the IRS? Taxpayers are going to tax courts, being railroaded and must prove their innocence. I think it is time for the politicians to stand up for the Constitution, tell the IRS they have the burden of proof, and if you accuse an American taxpayer, you have the burden of proof of coming in and proving the case. (*Congressional Record*, 1991, October 15, H7819)

This mission against the IRS is extremely personal as is the defense of John Demjanjuk. In both cases, Traficant has observed what he terms injustice, and his position in Congress has given him a medium to express that dissatisfaction.

In 1990 and 1991, there were two major events which brought James Traficant national exposure. The first was during the all night debate on the Federal budget. When the Federal buildings were in danger of being closed and budgets were in doubt in many areas, he yelled;

There are 200,000 troops over in the Persian gulf; 165,000 of them are Americans. This is a world problem. Let the world pay for it . . . . Our kids keep coming back in body bags, and our taxpayers keep financing it . . . . Let the United Nations work; 165,000 Americans is ridiculous. Let us get more people from other countries over there . . . . And I say, shut it down. It is better than crippling this Nation's freedom with a bad bill. (*Congressional Record*, 1990, October 4, H8925)

It is only through C-SPAN that the total impact of Traficant's words can be achieved. The exasperation in his voice and the strain being felt by other House members is captured by cameras, and provides much more information than the written text of Traficant's words.

A few days later, Traficant attempted to cut a Defense Appropriations Bill. He said,

. . . the trouble is, Congress does not own their vote anymore. Congress does not own their vote anymore. Congress sold out. This is a damn house of political prostitutes. I am not one of them . . . damn we have the best Congress that money can buy, I think. (*Congressional Record*, 1990, October 12, H9505-H9506)

Rep. David McCurdy (D-OK) chastised Traficant for his remarks and demanded an apology. Rep. Norman Dicks (D-WA) asked that Traficant's words be stricken from the record and "taken down," an unusual parliamentary move that denies the member's right to speak for the rest of the day.

Traficant did apologize to his colleagues on the Congressional floor and by personal letter a few days later. Interestingly, Traficant also corrected his usage in the *Congressional Record* for October 12. On C-SPAN he said, "Congress don't own its vote anymore. Congress don't own its vote anymore." Despite the slight change, this indicates the value of C-SPAN for capturing the informal flavor of the House proceedings that night.

In 1991, perhaps the most dramatic actions by Traficant on the House floor were tied to a series of parliamentary inquiries issued on June 7 and June 18. Both of these events were more vividly portrayed on C-SPAN than one could gain from reading the *Congressional Record*. On June 7, Traficant discovered a parliamentary loophole that allowed him to pressure committee members into accepting his "Buy American" amendment. On June 18, he used this loophole to the extreme. Hook & Hager (1991, June 29) called the appropriations bills debate "a procedural fiasco by a maverick Democrat" (1742). This power play by Traficant took every paragraph of the Treasury-Postal Service bill and called for a point of order. Hook and Hager called Traficant a "one man wrecking crew," but they did suggest that "it may haunt him if he ever again wants any spending for his district" (1743).

The cumulative effect of these types of demonstrations on the House floor via C-SPAN show the American people the frustration which affects both Congress and themselves alike. It also demonstrates the erosion of power of many of the long held seats on major committees in Congress. The 1992 primary election results are another indicator of the "old guard" being replaced. Issues such as the check bouncing scandals have cost many their long held seats in both houses of Congress. For example, the Illinois primary in March, 1992 unseated two major candidates who had held their positions for many years.

Now that we have examined Traficant's rhetoric and the historical context in which his public discourse occurs, we can shift to the critical analysis.

Analysis

Canovan (1981) examines the historical forms of populism from the farmer's movement in the 1890's through the Third World dictatorships, which she labels the politicians' populism of the twentieth century. She found two characteristics universally present. "All forms of populism without exception involve some kind of exaltation of and appeal to 'the people,' and all are in one sense or another antielitist" (294).

Traficant has been labeled "the working man's congressman." Morley Safer said, "Jim Traficant is Youngstown—tough, stubborn, mill-town through and through . . ." (1990, November 11). Lee (1986) discusses how populist rhetoric focuses on the individual, the agent. Traficant, for his constituents, is that agent, that "superperson."

Based on the responses to the two call in programs, Traficant has been well-received. Every caller on the July 11, 1991 program, professing to be both Republicans and Democrats, praised Traficant for his approach (ID# 18963). Traficant also exemplifies the anti-elitist stance. He does not conform to Washington's political norms of dress or decorum. For example, he won the "worst dressed" award in 1988 given by *The Washingtonian*. He claims openly that he has "killed a lot of polyesters" to make his clothes.

Lee (1986) sees two major functions of the new populist rhetoric. First, this rhetoric "intrumentalizes participation" (285). Traficant does this by participating in as much of Congressional activity as possible. In 1990 he did not miss one vote on the Congressional floor. Columnist, Jack Anderson, states, "only five percent of the nation's members of Congress can make such a boast" (1991, June 3, A7). Traficant exercises his Congressional privilege and addresses the floor for his "one minutes" nearly every session. He has become well-known for these speeches and sound bites from them frequently appear on evening news programs. Finally, Traficant tapes a half hour show in Washington and sends it to the ABC affiliate WYTV in Youngstown for airing each Sunday morning. As Foote (1991) has suggested, the politicians of the nineties have the political common sense to use the media to its fullest (1).

Second, Lee (1986) states that the new populist rhetoric rehabilitates radical opposition. "The discourse rehabilitates key political symbols and provides a rhetorical halfway house for those temporarily residing outside of 'official' politics" (286). In this Traficant excels. His rhetoric not only resides outside of traditional politics, it thrives on its opposition to those politics. Everything from Traficant's appearance to his ribald wit, defines him as an outsider. Even the *Vindicator* editorials say he is a "me vs. them" kind of politician. It is in this part of populism that Traficant has found his niche.

In an attempt to reconfigure rhetorical criticism as address to publics rather than public address, McKerrow (1989) sees the critic closely linked to the rhetor, carefully piecing together fragments of discourse to attempt to paint the picture of the rhetor's ideological vision. When examining Traficant's rhetoric, the bits and pieces of public discourse are gathered from multiple sources and reconstructed in such a way that the reader can see how many of the aspects of his life and discourse are interrelated. His "one minutes" alone can serve as forms of public address, but it is the analysis of letters to the editor, and network appearances with audience reactions, which often show the publics for which his rhetoric is intended.

One can argue that Traficant's rhetoric appeals simultaneously to multiple audiences. McKerrow argues that "fragments contain the potential for polysemic rather than monosemic interpretation" (107). This would explain populist appeal in general. Many members of Congress and the press have difficulty understanding Traficant's wide appeal, but his rhetoric is interpreted by different audiences in vastly different ways. Some are merely intrigued by his brash approach to other members of Congress. As Jack Anderson (1991) points out in his editorial, Traficant has people listening even if only to see what new antics he will pull (A7). This is an effective rhetorical ploy. Traficant may be lambasted by his colleagues, but they often vote on his amendments because he speaks the language of the overtaxed majority in the United States, the out-of-work laborers, and the underdogs, those struggling to survive. At the same time, Traficant speaks to the businesses in America which have suffered due to Japanese products putting them out of the competitive market. Each "Buy American" amendment submitted by Traficant brings positive responses from these publics. His political savvy has developed to the point where he has even forced committee members to vote on his amendments.

McKerrow (1989) identifies principles related to naming and absence, as key in building an ideology. The rhetor, in naming names, such as "Congress," "Japanese," and "IRS" has attached a label, providing a scapegoat for the argument. This process allows the audience to place its anger onto the scapegoat. This is what has brought Traficant accusations of racism and anti-Semitism, and Traficant seems to bask in the alienation. Even his calling Congress a house of "political prostitutes" is an example of this naming process.

This moves us to the concept of absence. Wander's (1984) discussion of "Third Persona" is closely tied with absence. The "Third Persona" is the unnamed and the undiscussed. It is the forgotten or unmentioned group; the process of hegemony whereby the group in power constrains the rhetoric or access to the rhetoric in such a way that the powerless group is never heard or discussed. The majority of Congress would not venture to discuss many of the subjects Traficant brings up on the House floor. His ridicule of members of Congress as "a bunch of wimps" and "political prostitutes" would be absent from most Congressperson's lips, as would most of the pleas to fund projects in Youngstown, Ohio. Traficant sees his mission as the spokesperson for these forgotten, these unmentioned and undiscussed. Even his powerplay on June 7 and 18, 1991 regarding the Treasury-Postal Service Bill was his way of addressing those forgotten steel and auto workers whose jobs have been lost and threatened in his area.

Canovan (1981) discusses the importance of "initiative, referendum, and recall" to the nineteenth century populist movement (173) and Traficant is reminiscent of these traditional populist rhetorical appeals. These three devices allowed the early populists to garner some moderate success. The threat of "recall," however slight, in this case, labels Traficant in that traditional populist way. The empowerment of the public is key to Traficant's ideology. This empowerment carries over to the Congress. Traficant has shown that he and many other members of Congress are powerless due to the long held seats on powerful committees. His parliamentary powerplay regarding the Appropriations committee's bill addresses that very issue (Hook & Hager, 1991, June 29).

Traficant, like Socrates, sees himself as the gadfly on the horse which is Washington, or more specifically, Congress. McKerrow looks at influence as opposed to causality as another aspect of ideological criticism. It would be foolhardy for Traficant, or his critic, to suggest that he can directly cause Congress to take one action over another. Traficant's anti-elitist approach is nothing new. In fact, Jack Anderson (1991) even suggests that if Traficant was speaking from the Congressional floor during the tumultuous sixties, he would have been just another one of many. These more conservative years in Washington have mellowed the radical bent of many once radical politicians and made the rhetorical gadfly not only unwelcome, but nearly as out of style as Traficant's skinny ties and bell bottom pants.

Conclusion

Traficant openly proclaims to be a thorn in the side of Congress. He is an astute politician, who does not merely pester other members of the House, but in many ways, says what others fear to say. The figures speak for themselves. James Traficant is being re-elected by his constituents. His public exposure has seemingly made him even more of a local hero, and, like it or not, Congress is beginning to act upon the legislation which he proposes. He has taken on many causes, and routinely attaches "Buy American" amendments to bills in Congress, using "one minutes" to attack Japanese trade practices, the OSI and their investigations of John Demjanjuk and Arthur Rudolph, taxes, and the IRS. From the days of defending himself in a racketeering trial and winning acquittal, to his claims that the Congress is a bunch of "political prostitutes," Traficant has basked in his alienation. When Don Hanni, the chairman of the Mahoning County Democratic party, was asked by Morley Safer what percent of Jim Traficant is an act. He replied, "I would say that Jim Traficant is probably 90 percent real, 10 percent or 5 percent an act and maybe 5 percent two cards short" (60 minutes, 1990, November 11).

Despite his antics on the Congressional floor, it is clear the James Traficant convinces his constituents back home. He receives a great deal of national exposure, and takes advantage of C-SPAN's public affairs coverage to make his voice heard. Traficant has a rhetorical style that makes the news. Time will tell whether his ideological vision can be sustained in the 17th Congressional District.

References

All area incumbents keep their seats (1990, November 7). *Vindicator*, B1.

Anderson, J. (1991, June 3). Rep. Traficant calls 'em. *Vindicator*, A7.

Foreign aid (1990, May 2). C-SPAN viewer call in. ID# 12106.

Budget resolution (1990, October 11). C-SPAN viewer call in. ID# 14456.

C-SPAN U.S. Japan relations simulcast, part I (1990, November 29). ID# 15166.

Trade issues (1991, July 11). C-SPAN viewer call in. ID# 18963.

Canovan, M. (1981). *Populism*. New York: Hartcourt Brace Jovanovich.

Cole, R. (1990, March 6). Area viewers cheer, praise performance. *Vindicator*, 1, 5.

Congressional Record (1987, March 11). Washington, DC: U.S. Government Printing Office, H1193.

Congressional Record (1990, September 13). Washington, DC: U.S. Government Printing Office, H7558.

Congressional Record (1990, September 18). Washington, DC: U.S. Government Printing Office, H7809-H7810.

Congressional Record (1990, October 4). Washington, DC: U.S. Government Printing Office, H8925.

Congressional Record (1990, October 12). Washington, DC: U.S. Government Printing Office, H9505-H9508.

Congressional Record (1991, March 20). Washington, DC: U.S. Government Printing Office, H1852.

Congressional Record (1991, May 21). Washington, DC: U.S. Government Printing Office, H2495.

Congressional Record (1991, October 15). Washington, DC: U.S. Government Printing Office, H7819.

Congressional Record (1991, November 22). Washington, DC: U.S. Government Printing Office, H10854.

Congressman defending scientist who is suspected in war crimes (1990, May 15). *New York Times*, A10.

De Souza, B. (1987, March 22). Traficant '3 Stooges' analogy on Contras draws limelight. *Vindicator,* A1, A10.

De Souza, B. (1990, June 28). Dubious honors Traficant shares 'Brain Dead'title. *Vindicator,* 1.

De Souza, B. (1990, July 25). Traficant speech fuels criticism. *Vindicator,* 1-2.

De Souza, B. (1990, October 12). Bishop also seeks Traficant's apology. *Vindicator,* 1, 4.

"Donahue: Congressman James A. Traficant, Jr." (1990, March 5). New York: Multimedia Entertainment.

"Donahue: Is America Falling Apart?" (1990, October 8). New York: Multimedia Entertainment.

Fiske, J. (1986). Television: Polysemy and popularity. *Critical Studies in Mass Communication, 3(4),* 391-408.

Foote, J. (1990, January 19). "Visibility" survey sings same song: You want TV time? Run for president. *Southern Illinois University News Service,* 1-3.

Foote, J. (1991, August 28). TV-Savvy congressmen snatch news coverage. *Southern Illinois University News Service,* 1-3.

Golden, K. M. (1991, November). *Congressman James A. Traficant, Jr.: A critical analysis.* Paper presented at the annual meeting of the Speech Communication Association, Atlanta, GA.

Goodall, J. (1990, March 6). Donahue, N.Y crowd back guest. *Vindicator,* 1, 5.

Hill, F. (1983). A turn against ideology: Reply to professor Wander. *Central States Speech Journal, 34(2),* 121-126.

Hook, J. & Hager, G. (1991, June 29). Appropriator's armor pierced in fast ride through house. *Congressional Quarterly,* 1742-1746.

How do others see the Mahoning valley? (1990, October 12). *Vindicator,* 14.

Lee, R. (1986). The new populist campaign for economic democracy: A rhetorical exploration. *Quarterly Journal of Speech, 72,* 274-289.

Lee, R. (1988). Moralizing and ideologizing: An analysis of political illocutions. *Western Journal of Speech Communication, 52,* 291-307.

Lee, R. & Andrews, J. R. (1991). A story of rhetorical-ideological transformation: Eugene V. Debs as liberal hero. *Quarterly Journal of Speech, 77,* 20-37.

McKerrow, R. E. (1989). Critical rhetoric: Theory and praxis. *Communication Monographs, 56,* 91-111.

Old Nazis, ageless crimes. (1991, May 21). *Wall Street Journal,* A23.

Sillars, M. O. (1991). *Messages, meanings, and culture: Approaches to communication criticism.* New York: Harper Collins.

"60 Minutes: Traficant" (1990, November 11). New York: CBS News.

Spiegel, L. B., Friedman, S. S., & Kutler, L. (1990, July 25). Traficant owes all apology for actions. *Vindicator,* 16.

Traficant and DeJulio race is simply no contest. (1990, November 4). *Vindicator,* C2.

Traficant reaches out to colleagues with letter of apology. (1990, October 20). *Vindicator,* 1.

Traficant relishes role as the ultimate outsider (1990, May 6). *Vindicator,* B3.

Traficant vote tally ranks among the highest (1988, November 15). *Vindicator,* 1-2.

Wander, P. (1983). The ideological turn in modern criticism. *Central States Speech Journal, 34(1),* 1-18.

Wander, P. (1984). The third persona: An ideological turn in rhetorical theory. *Central States Speech Journal, 35(4),* 197-216.

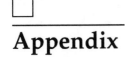

Appendix

Contact Information

C-SPAN Educational Services
Linda Heller, Director
400 North Capitol St., N.W.
Washington, D.C. 20001
(202) 737-3220
(800) 523-7586

Public Affairs Video Archives
Robert X Browning, Director
Purdue University
1025 Stewart Center
West Lafayette, IN 47907-1025
(317) 494-9630
(800) 423-9630
FAX: (317) 494-3421
BITNET: pava@purccvm

On-Air Program Schedule Times

C-SPAN provides an on-air programming at the following times:
Weekdays: 7:55 a.m., 6:25 p.m., 7:55 p.m. and 12:55 a.m.
Saturdays: 7:55 a.m., 6:55 p.m.
Sundays: 7:55 a.m., 7:55 p.m.
At quarter after and quarter before each hour, C-SPAN and C-SPAN 2 display schedule information at the bottom left hand corner of the television screen.

About the Authors

About the Editor

Janette Kenner Muir is assistant professor in the Communication Department at George Mason University, responsible for the direction of basic courses in public speaking, interpersonal communication and media literacy. Additionally, she teaches courses in rhetorical criticism and political communication. Muir has presented workshops on how to use C-SPAN in the classroom, and serves as a seminar leader for the C-SPAN in the Classroom Seminar for Professors held yearly in Washington, D.C. She is author of several articles and book chapters on political communication, and is currently researching call-in shows as forms of public empowerment.

About the Contributors

Jane Blankenship is professor in the Department of Communication at the University of Massachusetts, Amherst. She has published numerous books and essays about rhetoric and political communication. She is former president of the Speech Communication Association, and the Eastern Communication Association. She presently writes about women in politics.

Don M. Boileau is Chair of the Communication Department, and the director of Liberal Education for the College of Arts and Sciences, at George Mason University. He has served as parliamentarian for nineteen years for the Association of Teacher Educators, National Council of Teachers of English, College of Arts and Sciences, and other groups. He has published numerous essays on communication education.

Rod Carveth is associate professor in the Department of Mass Communication at the University of South Dakota. He is co-editor of *Media Economics: Theory and Practice*, and has authored a number of book chapters and articles on popular culture, and media effects.

Bruce E. Drushel is assistant professor in the Department of Communication at Miami University. He is author of several reviews and articles in mass communication journals and newsletters, and co-author (with Howard Frederick) of a chapter on U.S. international broadcasting in the recently published collection *Media in the Caribbean*.

Kathleen Golden is assistant professor in the Speech and Communication Studies Department at Edinboro University. Her research involves critical analyses of organizational, political, and religious discourse. She is an alumni of the "C-SPAN in the Classroom for Professors" Seminar.

Kenneth E. Hadwiger is professor in the Department of Communication Studies at Eastern Illinois University. He has taught and lectured in sixteen nations throughout Europe and Asia. Hadwiger has contributed articles on politics and mass communication to a variety of national and international journals. **Amy C. Paul** is a junior student intern of Communication at Eastern Illnois University. Her primary interests is in teacher education. She contributes as final editor of Hadwiger's essay.

Lawrence W. Hugenberg is professor of speech communication in the Department of Speech Communication and Theatre at Youngstown State University. He is the coordinator of the business and professional speaking course which enrolls over 1200 students annually. He is co-author of a business and professional speaking textbook, *Speaking in the Modern Organization: Skills and Strategies for Success* and is co-author of a simulations workbook, *Simulations for Business and Professional Communication*, which is in its 4th Edition.

Star A. Muir is assistant professor in the Communication Department at George Mason University. He is author of several articles on environmental communication and the discourse of technology. Currently, he is the editor of *Speaker and Gavel*, and the Policy Caucus Newsletter.

David R. Neumann is Chair of the Department of Communication at the Rochester Institute of Technology, New York. He has been teaching courses in persuasion for eight years and has recently produced a telecourse in the area. His research areas are diverse, ranging from teleconferencing to mental imagery.

Jim Schnell is associate professor of Communication at Ohio Dominican College in Columbus, Ohio. He was a visiting professor in 1987 and 1991 at Northern Jiaotong University in Beijing, The People's Republic of China, and visited south China in 1988. He is a Major in the Air Force Intelligence Command/Reserves (Pacific Command).

Craig Allen Smith is professor of Communication Studies at the University of North Carolina at Greensboro. He is author of *Political Communication*, co-editor of *The President and the Public: Rhetoric and National Leadership*, coauthor of *Persuasion and Social Movements*, and the forthcoming *The White House Speaks* as well as articles and book chapters on political communication.

Robert J. Snyder is assistant professor of Broadcast Journalism at the University of Northern Iowa. He has been a presenter at the C-SPAN Seminar for Professors in Washington, D.C.

Rita Kirk Whillock is assistant professor of Communication at Southern Methodist University. She is the author of *Political Empiricism: Communication Strategies in State and Regional Elections*. Whillock has also authored numerous essays relating to political persuasion.